AMERICAN HUMORS BEST ONE AND TWO LINERS

Allan D. Fisher

SHORT...HARD HITTING JOKES...
FOR ROTARY AND OTHER SERVICE
CLUBS...RETIREMENT AND
BIRTHDAY PARTIES...POLICE
AND FIREMAN GATHERINGS...

FOR ANYBODY WHO NEEDS TO
BE FUNNY IN FRONT OF A GROUP

Books by Allan D. Fisher

The Roast Book

Marinate The Cook

American Humors Best One and Two Liners

COPYRIGHT© 2002
ALLAN D. FISHER

All rights reserved. No part of this book may be reproduced in any form, except for the inclusion of brief quotations in a review, without permission in writing from the author or publisher.

Library of Congress Control Number: 2002112763

ISBN 0-9679951-1-6

Edited by Paul S. Thomsen
Photography by Ray Morris of San Francisco
First Edition December 2002

To order a book, for information on bulk purchases, or
for any additional information,
call Toll Free 1-866-625-4003
Or
You can order on our
Website www.sampsonbooks.com

Printed in the U.S.A. by
Sampson Publishing Company
268 Bush Street #907
San Francisco, CA 94104
1-866-625-4003

DEDICATION

To my son Mark. The best son a father could have. Thank you for all of your strength and support. Perhaps your greatest talent lies in the selection of your wife and having the three most wonderful grandchildren in the world! I love you,

Dad

TABLE OF CONTENTS

Age	1
Animals	8
Arkansas	10
Bachelor	11
Bald	11
Banker	12
Blacks	14
Cars	15
Cheap	16
Children	16
Christmas	20
Chubby	21
Closings	24
Computers	26
Consultant	26
Contractor	26
Cooking	27
Cop	28
Dentist	30
Divorce	30
Drinking	31
Dumb Blondes	34
Education	35
Environment	37
Executive	37
Family	39
Finance	41
Fund Raising	44
Gambler	44
General	45

Golf	51
Heckler Responses	54
Hunting-Fishing	55
Immigration	56
IncomeTax	57
Insurance	58
Introductions And Openings	58
Introverted-Quiet Person	71
Italian	73
Jewish	74
Ladies Man	76
Lawyers	79
Marriage	81
Medical	93
Mexicans	97
Military	97
Mother-in-Law	99
Movies	102
Musical	103
Newspapers	105
Optimist-Pessimist	105
Outfits	106
Pharmacist	108
Politics	108
Poor	116
Post Office	117
Promotion	118
Psychiatrist	118
Put Downs	119
Receiving An Award	132
Religion	133
Restaurants	138
Retirement	140

Rotary	142
Salesman	144
Seven-Eleven's	145
Sex	145
Shopping	150
Short	151
Speaker	152
Sports	154
Stock Broker	155
Tough Neighborhood	156
Travel	157
Ugly	158
Unlucky	159
Veterinarian	161
ABOUT THE AUTHOR	162

AGE

The formula for eternal youth is simple. Exercise, eat slowly (Pause), and lie about your age!

At his age, when he goes to the movies (Long pause) the only time a woman makes a pass at him (Pause) is to get his popcorn!

There are five signs of old age. The first is loss of memory. (Long pause) I can't remember the other four!

This is a man who goes out with younger women. (Pause) He has to. (Long pause) All the women his age are dead!

But now times have changed and Charlie is getting older. The other day he told me that his wife had given up sex for lent. (Long pause) And he didn't find out until Easter!

He went through high school in 8 years. Now it takes 12 years! He didn't have to take any history courses. In his day (Long pause), there was no history!

You know you're getting old when you're in a room full of women and instead of wondering which one has the best body, (Long pause) you wonder which one knows CPR!

Charlie is forever saying life is too short. Of course, it's too short (Pause) if you can only remember one third of it!

His back goes out more often than he does!

His social security number is twelve!

Now that I've reached sixty-five, when I sit down to eat at night I feel sexy. When I go to bed I feel hungry. (Pause) My life is upside down!

I saw an ad in the paper the other day. It said, "75-year-old man who drinks wants to meet a 75-year-old woman who drinks. Object — drinking!"

I'm really getting old! The other day I walked into a room and I couldn't remember why! (Long pause) And it was the bathroom!

My wife keeps telling me I'm interested in only one thing! And for the life of me (Long pause) I can't remember what that is!

My grandfather had the right idea. He died in his sleep. (Long pause) Not yelling and screaming like the others in his car!

This is a woman who knows what she's about! When she reached fifty, she knew exactly what she wanted to be! (Long pause) Thirty-five!

Charlie and I go back together a long way. We go back to a time when hot pants (Pause) was a condition! (Milton Berle)

Now that he has reached the golden years, Charlie is devoting himself to special projects. (Pause) Like trying to get the government to give discounts for massages!

He's marrying at seventy. (Long pause) And he's looking for a home near a school!

He's so old he brings Poligrip on dates, in case he wants to nibble on a girl's ear! (L. Page)

The girls still follow him. (Pause) But he can't remember why!

He keeps his waterbed full of Geritol!

I don't know how old Charlie is today. But I know Helen (Pause) won't even buy green bananas anymore!

I don't know how old Charlie is, but I know he must be up there. (Pause) His doctor makes him pay in cash for each visit!

Betty told us a surprising thing tonight. She told us that next year she is approaching 40. (Long pause) Everyone is wondering from which direction!

You know, Charlie, you look pretty good for a man your age! (Long pause) I don't care what everyone says!

I asked Charlie what he would like people to say about him 100 years from now. He said I would like them to say (Long pause), "He looks pretty good for his age!"

I asked Charlie what he considered happiness. He said "When your 80 years old and you are named in a paternity suit. (Long pause) And it's class action!"

By the way, Charlie, one of the members on this dais is almost as old as you are. (Long pause) And there are not a lot of people around who can say that!

When it comes to talking about her age, Betty is very shy. (Long pause) About 10 years shy!

Did you know that Betty was Miss America at the age of sixteen? (Long pause) Of course, there were very few Americans then!

She was named after Betty Davis, (or any other well-known person in past history whose first name is the same) (Long pause) not long after her either!

For those of you who missed the birthday cake lighting ceremony, it was really incredible. (Long pause) Looked like Mt. St. Helens with candles!

Her age is her own business. (Long pause) She's been in business a long time!

It takes him longer to rest than to get tired!

She say's he still chases girls (Pause), but only down hill!

Betty told me that the only reason she took up jogging (Long pause), was to hear heavy breathing again!

Have you ever noticed that old age comes at a bad time!

At Charlie's age, he's seen it all, done it all and heard it all. (Long pause) He just can't remember it all!

You know you are getting old when the candles cost more than the cake! (Bob Hope)

This man is old. At the Last Supper, he was a bus boy!

This was the first man ever (Pause), to assault a girl in a Stanley Steamer! (Dean Martin)

I don't know how old Betty is. But when she and her first husband got divorced, (Long pause) she got the cave!

His family told me when Cain killed Abel, (Pause) Charlie was on the jury!

At his age, the two most important things to him are sex and a few laughs. (Long, long pause). Unfortunately, (Pause) they come at the same time!

This is a man whose blood type has been discontinued!

He used to make tip money (Pause) parking covered wagons!

My grandmother is 88. She has a boy friend about the same age. (Long pause) They get along beautifully. (Pause) They can't hear each other!

My eyes are going but thank God I can still clean my teeth! (Long pause) It's easy when you can hold them in your hand! (Alan King)

Earlier this evening we caught him sniffing the prunes! (Dean Martin)

The other night my wife said, "Let's go upstairs and make love." I said, (Pause) "Hon, pick one or the other, (Long pause) we can't do both?"

Never, never, (Long pause) pass up the opportunity to go pee!!!

Old is when the term, "Getting a little action" means (Long pause) I don't need to take any fiber today!

It took years. Now I have finally got my head together, (Long pause) and my body is falling apart!

I used to focus on the Rolling Stones. (Long pause) Now, (Pause) it's the kidney stones!

You talk about frustration! By the time I got to the right place at the right time, (Long pause) I was at the wrong age!

Charlie you have just got to slow down. (Pause) You're not a a spring chicken anymore. (Long pause) And according to your wife (Pause) you're not much of a rooster either?

How do you make an 85-year-old woman say the "F" word? (Long pause) Get another 85-year-old woman to yell, (Pause) "Bingo!"

This woman was born in the year of our Lord, (Long Pause) only knows!

I responded to one of those TV ads and sent in $19.95 for an album of oldies but goodies. (Long pause) They sent me a nude picture of Mae West!

I went to a cocktail party at the Senior Center the other night. (Long pause) That is the first time I have ever seen a martini (Pause) served with a prune!

I'm not sure how old she is. (Long pause) But she knew Howard Johnson when he only had two flavors!

In female circles, (Pause) he's known as a WOW. (Long pause) A worn-out-wolf!

I'm so old (Pause) I can remember when people who wore blue jeans (Long pause) worked!

I know your old Charlie, but the good news is (Long pause) you're on this side of the grass!

I finally reached the age when I have all the answers. But now, (Long pause) nobody asks me the questions!

Charlie has proved once again (Pause) that there is no fool like an old fool. (Long pause) You just can't beat experience!

Charlie's mind works pretty fast. He forgot his wife's birthday and he said to her, "How do you expect me to remember your birthday (Long pause) when you never look any older?"

In his day, wonder drugs (Pause) were mustard plaster and caster oil!

This is a woman who has what it takes. (Long, long pause) But she's had it so long (Pause) nobody wants it!

I'm not sure how old she is, (Long pause) but her first husband was captain of the Mayflower!

She started out as a dreamboat. (Long pause) But now her anchor drags and her cargo shifted!

I think her age is like the speedometer on a used car. You know it's set back (Pause) but you don't know how far!

I guess I'm getting old. I don't care where my wife goes (Long pause) as long as I don't have to go with her!

ANIMALS

Do you know what you call a Scotsman with six or more sheep? (Long pause) A pimp!

I've heard people say that a dog is your best buddy! Think about that! (Pause) How many of your best buddies have you had neutered this month?

This is a guy who loves animals! He loves his dog. (Pause) He loved his dog so much, that he married her! (Long, long pause) He had to!

Hey, some days you're the dog. (Long pause) Some days you're the hydrant!

Penguins mate for life. (Pause) That doesn't really surprise me. They all look exactly alike. It's not like they're gonna meet a better-looking penguin someday! (Ellen DeGeneres)

My dog is lazy. He doesn't chase cars. (Pause) He sits on the curb and takes down license plate numbers! (Rodney Dangerfield)

I once had a dog that really believed he was man's best friend. (Long pause) He kept borrowing money from me. (Gene Perret)

People think alligators are stupid! Not true! (Long pause) They eat their young!

He sleeps with his dog. The scratching doesn't bother him. (Long pause) Well, (Pause) the dog has gotten used to it!

I had bad luck with pets. (Long pause) I even had to send my turtle to obedience school!

When you go to Yellowstone National Park, the first thing you learn, (Pause) is never pat a bear on the head. (Long pause) Otherwise, (Pause) the last thing you learn, (Pause) is never pat a bear on the head!

I have this dog that doesn't do tricks or anything. Actually, (Long pause) he's an obedience school drop out!

Los Angeles is the only city in the world where the lions in the zoo are kept behind bars. Not for your protection, (Long pause) but for theirs!

The University of California at Davis has tested and proved that one of the donkeys that Charlie has on his farm has an I. Q. of 134, but the other donkeys won't have anything to do with him. Well (Long, long pause) nobody likes a smart ass!

One of Charlie's pigs took sick so he gave him some sugar. I said, "Why did you give him sugar?" He said, (Long pause) "You never heard of sugar-cured ham?"

He bred his dog with a pig. (Long pause) Now he has a pet that fetches garbage!

He crossed a porcupine and a gorilla. I'm not sure what he got. (Long pause) But when it rides on the subway, (Pause) it sits anywhere it wants!

Charlie ran an ad in the paper offering a reward of $500.00 for the return of his wife's cat. I said, "Charlie, that's a lot of money." He said, "Not for this one. (Long pause) I drowned it!"

I said, "Charlie, does your dog have a good pedigree? He said, "Good pedigree, (Long pause) if he could talk he wouldn't speak to either of us!

I asked the zookeeper, "Are those monkeys playing poker?" He said, "Yes, (Long pause) but they only play for peanuts!"

Monkeys are wonderful animals because they have such a good time because there's so many of them. (Long pause) And there's so many of them (Long pause) because they have such a good time!

I got a dog for my wife. (Long, long pause) Best trade I ever made!

ARKANSAS

In Arkansas they passed a new law. Even when couples get divorced, (Pause) they're still brother and sister!

Arkansas is very proud of Bill Clinton. (Long pause) All these women coming forward (Pause) and none of them is his sister!

O. J. Simpson wanted to move to Arkansas (Pause) because everyone has the same DNA!

BACHELOR

It was Charlie who said, "Always get married in the morning. So, if it doesn't work out (Pause) you haven't shot the whole day!"

We used to call people who didn't like to fight cowards. (Pause) Today we call them bachelors!

He likes being a bachelor. He gets to have a home cooked meal any time he wants. (Long pause) And he even gets to pick the cook!

He had such a good time at his bachelor party that (Long pause) he cancelled the wedding. (Long pause) He had to!

BALD

At night, (Pause) his head slips off the pillow!

I see a lot of bald people in the crowd tonight. Well, just remember, (Long pause) they don't put marble tops on cheap furniture!

Charlie's mother always said he'd come out on top, (Long pause) and by God he has!

Here I am introducing the guy who looks like the melon I had for breakfast!

I don't care what they say about baldness. You gotta admit, (Long pause) it's neat!

Life is a series of unfulfilled dreams. For instance, Charlie always wanted to wear his hair long, (Long pause) at least a lot longer than he did!

He's not bald (Pause) he's just too tall for his hair!

At least he found the perfect cure for dandruff!

A lot of people have problems with split hair (Run your hand over your hair) (Long, long pause) Charlie's hair split about ten years ago!

(Stare at Charlie) You can all see that Charlie is a man of polish! (Continue to stare)

BANKER

He started out his banking career as a Teller. He loved it. (Long pause) He was bringing home $180,000 a week!

It's hard for me to believe that bankers are good at counting. If they're so good, (Pause) why do they have 12 teller windows (Pause) and two tellers?

He's reached a point in his life that he would much prefer to hear his banker say yes, (Pause) then his girlfriend!

It seems to be a mystery where Charlie got the money to start this bank. Oh, he's still insured, (Long, long pause) but you have to go to Sicily to get it!

I learned one thing about banks. The guy who writes the newspaper ads (Long pause) is not the same guy who makes the loans!

I asked him what the name of his bank was. He said, (Long pause) "Piggy!"

He didn't join the bank's Christmas club this year. (Long pause) He couldn't attend all the meetings!

When it comes to savings, banks are okay. But what we really need, (Long pause) is a mattress that pays 8%!

This woman loves America. She loves everything about America. She loves the songs of America, (Pause) the people of America and primarily, (Long pause), she loves the Bank of America!

Charlie borrowed some money from his bank. Once the deal was completed, he told his banker he needed an additional $5,000. (Long pause) He bet his buddy $5,000 he wouldn't get the loan!

His kid's piggy bank has a vice president!

He started out as a cashier (Long pause) in a piggy bank!

He started out as a teller (Long pause) in a blood bank!

BLACKS

Charlie (a black man) saw the movie "Roots." So he went to Africa to search for his roots. (Long pause) He traced them all the way back to Detroit! (Milton Berle)

(A good line to use on a Black, Hispanic or Jewish person) Charlie is a member of one of the city's largest minority groups. (Long pause) He is a Democrat!

I said to Charlie, "What would you do if you got a letter from the Klu Klux Clan telling you to get out of town!" He said, (Long pause) " I'd read it on the bus!"

It was Charlie's grandfather, the first black soldier in World War II who said, (Pause) "Don't shoot until you see the whites!"

Charlie claims his ancestors were the first black family to land on Plymouth Rock. (Long pause) And they immediately threw it through the window of the general store!

Looking at this dais, (Pause) I haven't seen this much white (or dark) meat since my Thanksgiving turkey blew up! (Redd Foxx)

I said to my friend, "Do you think a black can ever become president of the United States?" He said, "Yes, (Long pause) if he runs against a Mexican!"

(To use after a black speaker has sat down) Once again, Charlie, you have proved that black is beautiful. (Long pause) Not funny, but beautiful! (Dean Martin)

This is the only black man in the country (Pause) without his own situation comedy!

(To a black man) I had to teach him the shuffle. (Long pause) You know these people don't have any rhythm!

Hey, just go to Harlem and walk through the hospital zone. (Long pause) Anywhere you walk in this zone (Pause) you're going to the hospital! (Nippsy Russell)

This is a man who orders fried chicken seven days a week, (Long pause) so he can build up frequent fryer meals!

CARS

I bought a Japanese car. I turn on the radio. (Pause) I don't understand a word they're sayin! (Rodney Dangerfield)

Remember ladies (Long pause) if it has tires or testicles, sooner or later (Long pause) you're going to have trouble with it!

My new car has something that will last a lifetime. (Long pause) Monthly payments!

Buick has come up with a new sports car and they're calling it, "Congress." Sounds good, (Long pause) but it can't pass anything!

Have you seen his car? If he decided to buy a skateboard, (Long pause) he'd be trading up!

I bought my car from old Bill over here and I got a 10-year guarantee on the drive shaft. (Long pause) That's got to be the longest shaft in the history of car sales!

This man took the engine from a Mercedes, the chassis from a Chrysler and fenders from a Ford and do you know what it got him? (Long pause) Four years!

CHEAP

What a cheapskate that guy is. His wife wanted a foreign convertible. (Long pause) He got her a rickshaw!

At the Last Supper, (Long pause) he would have asked for separate checks!

Some people think of Charlie as conservative. (Pause) Some people think of Charlie as frugal. Most of us, (Pause) think of Charlie as cheap!

It's fitting that we give Charlie a dinner. Everyone does! (Long pause) He hasn't picked up a check in years!

CHILDREN

The best way to drive a baby buggy (Long pause) is to tickle its feet!

They have really good looking kids. Can you believe that? (Long pause) It's a good thing she cheats!

I told my kid. Look, this is not just my house! It's your house too! (Long, long pause). He sold it!

Children are the curse of marriage!

The only indication I have ever had that my son could keep his mind on two things at the same time, (Long pause) is his poster of Dolly Parton!

You used to put your kids to sleep at night with bedtime stories. Now they come in at bedtime (Pause) and tell you stories that keep you awake all night long!

I'll say this! My wife really raised our kids by the book. (Long pause) I think it was Peyton Place!

"Now Junior," said the teacher, "A little birdie told me that you swear." The kid says, (Long pause) "It musta been one of them damned sparrows!"

Have you noticed how kids are always complaining? To a five-year-old, nothing is ever right. He's like (Long pause) Ralph Nader with a runny nose!

Kids are unbelievable. (Pause) My daughter today is reading books that twenty years ago would have embarrassed our family doctor!

His mother said, "You know, it was nice of you to let your little sister use the ice skates first." Charlie said, "Yes, (Long pause) I wanted to find out if the ice was too thin!"

Have you seen any of these new first grade readers? They're all about Jane, Dick and Spot. Spot is a dog. (Long pause) Jane is nothing to brag about either!

My son has one of those haircuts that cover his eyes, ears, nose and neck. If the barber is busy, (Pause) we take him to the vet!

Should women have children after 35? (Long pause) No, 35 children are enough!

One of the greatest mysteries of life is how the idiot who married your daughter, (Long pause) can be the father of the smartest grandchildren in the whole world!

Having kids is like having a bowling alley installed in your head!

Charlie's parakeet died the other day. Well, the grandchildren were over and they were playing badminton! (Long, long pause) It was ugly!

In a nutshell, be good and kind to your children. Not only are they the future of the world, (Long pause) they are the ones who will sign you into the home!!!

I can stand here tonight and tell you truthfully that one of my kids made me a millionaire! (Long pause) Of course, (Pause) I was a multimillionaire before he got started!

I finally figured out a way to be sure the baby sitter kept an eye on the baby. (Long pause) I left it in the refrigerator!

Right next door to us the kids are in trouble all the time. And it's because of who they hang out with. (Long pause) Their parents!

I sent my kid to one of those summer camps that's run strictly by the book. (Long pause) My checkbook!

His kids have really been acting up. (Long pause) He goes to P.T.A. meetings under an assumed name!

When my son got married, he asked me how far apart children should be spaced. (Long pause) I said, (Pause) "About one mile!"

Charlie's kids were really problem children. When they were in school (Long pause) six teachers (Pause) offered to pay for Charlie's vasectomy!

I was taking my grandson to school the other day and he said, "Grandpa, before you married Grandma, (Long pause) who told you how to drive!"

Bedtime stories have been given a modern twist. The other day I heard one that goes, "Once upon a time there was a mama bear, a papa bear and a baby bear (Long Pause) by a previous marriage!"

The Geography teacher asked, "Does anyone know where St. Louis is? A voice in the back of the room yells, (Long pause) "They're playing in New York!"

Charlie almost had a heart attack. When the nurse came out of his wife's delivery room he said, "Is it a boy?" She said, (Long pause) "The one in the middle is!"

CHRISTMAS

For Christmas, he gave all his girl friends the same thing. (Long pause) Herpes!

People on my street put out so many Christmas tree lights anymore, I'm not sure if we're celebrating the birth of Jesus (Long pause) or General Electric!

Our office Christmas party got away from us this year. The office manager had a new carol, (Long pause) "Check The Halls For Saul and Molly!"

If you really want to brighten up your life, make a deal with your wife not to exchange Christmas presents this year. (Long pause) And then don't!

My wife is very emotional about the Christmas gifts I give her. She likes to get something I've created myself. (Long pause) I think this year (Long pause) I'll give her an ulcer!

I've finally decided what Christmas gift to give the girl in my neighborhood that has everything. (Long, long pause) Me!

This past Christmas I got myself one of those advanced new educational toys. (Long pause) Unfortunately, (Long pause) my wife found out about her!

For Christmas, (Pause) he gave a nudist a pocket watch!

CHUBBY

Just imagine how the world would be if there were no men! Think about it! No crime! Just a bunch of happy, (Pause) fat women!

I don't know if you have noticed her dress lately, but she is becoming far more fashionable. (Long pause) It's nice to see them putting style into larger sizes!

If you think he's big, you ought to see his brother. (Long pause) His brother looks like something that got loose from the Macy's Thanksgiving Day parade!

This is a guy whose daddy had to put truck tires on his bike!

She was voted Miss Nevada, (Long, long pause) Miss Idaho and parts of Montana!

I watched him put sunscreen on, (Long pause) with a roller!

I won't say that Charlie's too heavy, but if you browned him a little, (Pause) the Argentine army could feed off him for a year!

Watching him eat reminds me of feeding time at the zoo!

He has more chins then a Chinese phone book!

Charlie recently returned from 3 weeks in Europe, fighting diet problems all the way. The doctor put him on a 7-day diet. (Long pause) He ate the whole thing in one meal!

She missed being Miss America by two feet. (Long pause) Twelve inches on each hip!

The stork didn't deliver him. (Long pause) He came in a U-haul!

His first day at school, he became a dropout. (Long pause) The floor gave out under him!

I don't know how we can even begin to roast Charlie tonight. (Pause) I'm not even sure we could get him in the oven!

His mother called him (Pause) Butterball!

A group of Texas businessmen just bought him! (Long pause) They plan to tear him down and put up a Marriott Hotel!

I see my buddy Charlie is here tonight! He really looks uncomfortable! (Long pause) He could give birth any minute!

Your Mama is so fat——she gets group insurance!

Your Mama is so fat——she was born on the 2nd, 3rd and 4th of May!

They say inside every fat man there is a thin man trying to get out! (Long pause) In his case there are 8 thin men trying to get out!

I'm not saying she spends a lot of time in the supermarket. But last week, (Long pause) she took her shopping cart in for a 10,000 mile checkup!

She is a really big woman. (Pause) She has calves (Long pause) that only a cow could love!

Charlie went to one of those diet doctors and in just 60 days (Long pause) he lost $1,500!

This is a woman who is pretty well reared. (Long, long pause) I guess I could have phrased that differently!

He went on a diet (Long pause) but he got thick and tired of it!

Charlie's doctor told him to watch his waistline. (Long pause) (Pat your stomach) He put it right out there where he could keep an eye on it!

He's the only guy in the room (Long pause) who can get in to his side of the bed, (Pause) from either side!

If she puts on ten more pounds, (Pause) the state will make her wear license plates!

She ran out of a store in a yellow dress (Pause) and three guys yelled, "Taxi!"

She's always been considered a light eater. (Long pause) As soon as it gets light, she starts eating!

Every time she turns around (Long pause) she rearranges the furniture!

In her graduation picture, (Pause) she was the front row!

She is five feet tall. (Long pause) In any direction!

CLOSINGS

And now in closing, and when a Methodist (Or whatever denomination fits.) says in closing, (Long pause) he doesn't necessarily mean right now!

As for this evening, (Long pause) I've enjoyed every week of it!

I think that everyone in this room would agree. Charlie, you are the best at what you do. (Long pause) We only wish we knew what the hell that was!

And now, in the immortal words of Brigadier General George Armstrong Custer, (Long pause) "Let's get the hell out of here!"

I want to thank you all for this wonderful evening. I will remember it, (Long pause) until I get out of the parking lot!

I want to thank all of you on the dais tonight for making me feel at home. (Long pause) And frankly I wish I were there right now! (Hubert Humphrey)

People have asked questions about what I stand for. (Long pause) Well after tonight (Long pause) you can see I stand for a lot! (Barry Goldwater)

Tradition dictates that I now introduce our honoree and give him the last word! On the other hand, (Long pause) tradition has no idea just how dull this guy is!

I laughed at all your jokes tonight. (Long pause) Well, somebody had to laugh!

(When you introduce the guest of honor after he has been roasted) Now I'm going to introduce the case for the defense!

(When you introduce the guest of honor after he has been roasted) Charlie, may you live forever. (Pause) And may the last voice you hear (Pause) be mine!

I didn't think it was possible for this group to get together and say funny things about me for an hour. (Long pause) I was right! (Dennis Weaver)

(When you introduce the guest of honor after he has been roasted) Now, we're going to take one more look at the body, (Pause) and then we're going to close the lid!

I'm not used to telling jokes in public. (Long pause) And it's obvious that none of you are either! (Bill Conrad)

As Henry the Eighth said to each of his six wives, (Long pause) " I won't keep you very long!"

Well I think I'll close out my remarks. I remember the advice the mama whale gave her baby. "Only when your spouting (Pause) are you likely to get harpooned!"

Well I think it's time to quit. Like my friend Charlie who walked into a bar, ordered five shots, downed them one right after another and passed out. The bartender said, "That's what I like about Charlie, (Long pause) he knows when to quit!

I see we have some optimists in the crowd. An optimist is a fellow who puts his shoes back on when the speaker says, "And in conclusion!"

COMPUTERS

Computers can never completely replace humans. They may become capable of artificial intelligence, (Pause) but they will never master real stupidity!

The great thing about computers is that there are just as many mistakes as ever. (Long pause) But now, it's nobody's fault!

My life is really confused. I woke up at 2:00 AM to go to the bathroom (Long pause) and I checked my E-Mail on the way back to bed!

CONSULTANT

You all know what a consultant is. That's a guy who knows 49 different ways to make love, (Long pause) but doesn't have a girl friend!

A consultant is a person who can tell you more about something than you really care to know!

A consultant is the average guy (Pause) 20 miles out of town!

CONTRACTOR

Charlie is a real craftsman. You might say a dedicated carpenter. (Long pause) He's usually hammered!

Charlie is a plumber who really rubs it in. (Pause) I mean, who wears mink overalls?

What a guy he is. For Christmas he gave his electrician (Long pause) some shorts!

COOKING

My wife is one of the great cooks of our time. Do you know what she made last night? (Long pause) A reservation!

You have no idea how my wife's relatives can eat. One year I bowed my head to say grace and when I looked up, (Pause) somebody was handing me an after dinner mint!

My mother served me leftovers every night of my life until I left home. (Long pause) There was never an original meal!

My wife took a full year of Home Economics classes. (Long pause) The only thing she learned (Long pause) was how to call Pizza Hut!

Do you want to know how good a cook this guy is? (Pause) Last week he won the National Pillsbury Bake-Off (Long, long pause) with a Betty Crocker recipe!

When I was a kid, my mother fed us so many TV dinners (Pause) that every time I see aluminum foil, (Long pause) I get hungry!

A chef is the individual in the kitchen (Pause) who has a big enough vocabulary to give the soup a different name each day!

COP

A large woman came up to a policeman and said, "Could you see me across the street?" The policeman replied, (Long pause) "Lady, I could see you in Honolulu!"

My wife was stopped for speeding so many times, (Long pause) that the cops gave her a season ticket!

He's a brave man! He recently took quite a beating while fighting for a woman's honor. (Long pause) It seems she wanted to keep it!

The other day, Charlie learned something about the police that he didn't know. (Long Pause) He found out the city also pays them!

This is Betty's cousin twice removed. (Long pause) Once by the local police and once by the F.B.I.!

Boy, crime is rampant in this town. My wife sent me into the store the other day to get a pair of nylon stockings, (Long pause) and they wanted to know my head size!

My beat is located in a really tough neighborhood. The other night I went to the A.T.M. machine and the receipt said, (Long pause) "Run dummy run!"

In Detroit, (Any city you choose) two-thirds of the people say they will never move out of the city, (Long pause) unless of course their probation officer agrees to it!

When Betty joined the police department, the very first job they gave her set the tone for her career. They sent her to the airport, (Long pause) to sniff luggage!

So Charlie says to the cop, "What do you mean my eyes are glassy? Your eyes are clear. What have you been drinking, (Pause) Windex?"

Crime is so bad in this city that if you're not home by 9:00 PM, (Pause) you can be declared legally dead! (Dean Martin)

Charlie was working the riot in Watts when a brother came out of the furniture store with a couch on his back. Charlie said, "Are you a looter?" The guy said, "No, (Pause) I'm a psychiatrist on a house call!" (Nippsy Russell)

Chief, some of your friends couldn't be here tonight to honor you. However, we did receive this telegram from the Gay Liberation Movement. "Dear Chief Jones, we appreciate your efforts——but then we always admire someone who gets their man!" (Dean Martin)

Mr. Security. Here's a guy who wears both a belt and suspenders. (Long pause) On his pajamas!

I had a cousin who was a psychic! He even knew the day he was going to die! (Long pause) The warden told him!

I asked our chief what he would do if he had to arrest his own wife? He said, (Long pause) "Call for a back up!"

A young girl called the police station and told the desk sergeant that last week she had been assaulted. He asked her why she waited a week to call and the girl told him she didn't know she had been assaulted (Long pause) until the check bounced!

DENTIST

I once belonged to a union that had a dental plan. If you paid your dues, (Pause) you got to keep your teeth!

I told Charlie my teeth were turning yellow and asked him what I could do. He said, (Long pause) "Wear a brown tie!"

I don't understand. Every time I go to my dentist, he tells me not to pick my teeth with any sharp objects. (Pause) Then he spends the next hour doing just that!

My dentist pulls out an 8-inch needle and says, "This will help with the pain!". (Long Pause) That didn't sound right!

Charlie went in to his dentist the other day and he was sitting in the dental chair counting his money. The dentist said, "Oh, you don't have to pay me now." Charlie said, "Pay you? (Pause) I'm counting my money before you give me the gas!"

DIVORCE

This man filed for divorce the morning after his wedding. The morning after! It makes no sense! (Long pause) I mean how bad could breakfast have been?

It was an equitable divorce. A 50-50-property split. (Long pause) She got the house and he got the mortgage!

He has decided that rather than get married again, he's simply going to find a woman he doesn't like (Long pause) and give her a house!

DRINKING

When I first met her, she told me it only took one drink to get her drunk. What she didn't tell me was (Long pause) it was drink #8 that did it!

What a guy. For her birthday he bought something for the house. (Long pause) A round of drinks!

They found an olive in his blood test!

His whole family is drinkers! When his grandfather died, he was cremated! (Long pause) Took 3 days to put out the fire!

The doctor gave him one day to stop drinking. (Long pause) He picked January 10, 2009!

He's half Irish and half Scotch. Half of him wants to drink. (Long pause) The other half doesn't want to pay for it!

Did you ever notice? He looks like he was bombed before Pearl Harbor!

Charlie's hometown was so moral, they didn't even have a town drunk. Each day, (Pause) the men of the town had to take turns! (Jimmy Stewart)

The other night he drank so much corn liquor (Pause) we had to shuck him to get him in bed!

There's one thing about being out socially with Charlie. Here's a man who knows his limit. (Long pause) He's never been able to reach it (Pause) but at least he knows what it is!

Charlie told me the other day that excessive drinking destroys either your liver or your memory. (Long pause) He couldn't remember which one!

He has no respect for age, (Long pause) unless it's bottled!

Charlie saw a sign that said "Drink Canada Dry." (Pause) So, he went up there!

The only thing that ever sobered him up, (Long pause) was the check!

Charlie is really cool under pressure. The only time I ever saw him get upset was last Thursday, (Pause) when someone stole the cork out of his lunch!

Betty said, "Will you stop drinking for me?" Charlie said, "What makes you think I was drinking for you?"

I've heard about blackouts before, (Pause) but between 1967 and 1983?

Charlie was arrested for feeding straight bourbon to his pet bird. He was charged with (Long pause) contributing to the delinquency of a myna!

Here's a guy who has seen Dawn more often than Tony Orlando!

The shortest book I ever read was, (Pause) "A Guide To Dry Counties In Ireland!"

We call him a light drinker. (Long pause) He drinks until it gets light!

He speaks Scotch. (Long pause) With a soda accent!

I drank to his health so often (Pause) I ruined mine!

This is a bright girl. (Long pause) Always lit!

Charlie was sitting in a bar. A horse walks in and sits down on the stool next to him. The bartender says, (Long pause) "Why the long face?"

He quit AA and joined Triple A! (Pause) Now they tow him out of bars! (Totie Fields)

Despite what you've heard, this man doesn't have a drinking problem. (Pause) As long as the bars are open!

Being the designated driver is a lousy job. If you ever have to do it, at least have some fun with it. At the end of the night, (Long pause) drop them off at the wrong house! (Jeff Foxworthy)

This guy's list of "Most Admired People" (Pause) includes Jack Daniel's!

Talk about drinking. He falls down in his front yard so often (Long pause) the neighbors think he's a lawn ornament!

A woman drove me to drink. (Long pause) And I have never ceased to thank her! (W. C. Fields)

Do you know the difference between a coconut and a Scotchman? (Long pause) You can get a drink out of a coconut!

DUMB BLONDES

This woman isn't a dumb blond. (Long pause) I've seen her roots!

There's only 3 ways you can become a blond. On your mother's side, on your father's side, (Pause) or on peroxide!

A blond, a redhead and a brunette were all in the fifth grade. Which one had the biggest breasts? (Long pause) The blond, (Pause) because she was 18!

What do you call a smart blond? (Long pause) A Golden Retriever!

Dolly Parton released a statement to the press indicating that she was not offended by all the dumb blond jokes because she knows she's not dumb. (Long pause) Of course, (Pause) she also knows she's not a blond!

I walked right up to her and I said, "Gentlemen prefer blonds!" She smiled and said, (Pause) "I'm not really a blond!" I said, "Well that works out fine, (Long pause) because I'm not really a gentleman!"

Talk about a social blunder. I said to an old friend I hadn't seen in a while, "What happened to that stupid blond you used to run around with?" His wife said, (Long pause) "I dyed my hair!"

EDUCATION

Charlie shined in history. One day the teacher asked, "What was Gandhi's first name?" Charlie says, (Pause) "Goosey Goosey!"

Charlie told me he is really concerned about the level of education at his son's high school. He said the senior voted most likely to succeed, (Long pause) didn't graduate!

In college he majored in Animal Husbandry. (Long pause) Until one day they caught him at it!

Charlie can still remember his college days, (Long pause) both of them!

I'm only kidding about PhDs. It's like I was telling the cab driver on my way over here. I said, (Long pause) "Doctor, (Pause) it's the next corner!"

I don't understand it. In Elementary School, in case of fire, you line up in single file from the smallest to the tallest. (Long pause) Do tall people burn slower?

What a progressive school superintendent we have. (Long pause) The finger painting class, (Pause) uses a nude model!

When I graduated from college, I'm not going to tell you which half of the class I was in. (Long pause) But I was in the group that made the top half possible!

You heard about the riot they had the other day at the high school because the kids said the food was so bad. (Pause) They broke down a door, (Long pause) with a sausage!

Abraham Lincoln used to walk miles and miles just to borrow books to further his education. So in celebration of his birthday, (Long pause) we close the schools!

If my kid got as much out of college as he got out of me, (Pause) he'll do okay!

I told my kid, "When Abraham Lincoln was your age, he walked 20 miles to school and studied by the light of a fire in his log cabin." The kid said, "When John Kennedy was your age (Long pause) he was President!"

When Charlie was in high school, his counselor told him that his aptitude tests clearly indicated (Long pause) that his best opportunities lie in a field (Long pause) where his father had considerable influence!

Our superintendent of schools spends virtually all his time focused on his three major problems. Salaries for the teachers— football for the alumni— parking space for the students!

My kid went to a progressive college. No tests, pick any subject, pick any teacher, and use any books you want. (Long pause) But now she's living in a $400,000 house! (Long, long pause) Mine! (Pause) Nobody will hire her!

ENVIRONMENT

Talk about the environment. Last week a river in New York caught fire! (Long pause) What do they put it out with?

The air pollution in Los Angeles is terrible. I went through L. A. last week and had the guy in the gas station put air in my tires. (Long pause) Two of them died!

EXECUTIVE

People say he's a man of vision. Last night he dreamed that he ate a 5-lb. marshmallow. (Long pause) When he woke up, (Pause) his pillow was gone!

I don't know how many times I've seen this man with his shoulder to the wheel and his nose to the grindstone! (Long pause) It's not easy sleeping like that!

Some of you may not know this but Charlie left the first job he had due to illness. (Long pause) The boss got sick of him!

Charlie runs his company with an iron fist. I mean an iron fist! His contract states that if he dies, (Long pause) they bury one of the vice presidents!

When you look back at his career and all the great decisions that made him so successful, you can sum it all up in one word. (Long pause) Lucky!

This is an executive with vision! At every meeting, (Long pause) he always starts the bull rolling!

An executive is a person who is always early when you're late (Pause) and late when you're early!

Charlie told me he was really starting to get concerned about the rat race. He said he didn't know if he was slowing up, (Long pause) or they were bringing up faster rats!

He said he was more and more concerned about the rat race. Particularly when the rat about to pass you (Pause) is wearing high heels!

Charlie is a very organized executive. Every morning he goes into his office and makes out two lists. Things to do, (Long pause) and people to do them to!

Charlie is an executive who has always been able to find time to listen to our problems, (Long pause) and then add to them!

Charlie is an executive. An executive is the man who talks with visitors, (Pause) so the other employees can get the work done!

This is an executive who never makes the same mistake twice. (Long pause) Each day, (Pause) he manages to find some new mistake to make!

Charlie has discovered something that does the work of ten men. (Long pause) Ten women!

But Charlie is a true executive. Executive, that's a guy who delegates all the authority, (Pause) shifts all the blame, (Pause) and takes all the credit!

Charlie refers to his fellow executives as family. At least I think he does! (Long pause) He always calls them Mothers!

Charlie runs a non-profit company. It wasn't supposed to be. (Long pause) It's just worked out that way!

What an employee this guy has been. This year he used up all his sick leave. The last couple of months, (Long pause) he's been calling in dead!

I don't know how much of a contribution he makes to our company, (Long pause) but I understand his paychecks are coming gift-wrapped!

Charlie had a peach of a secretary. (Long pause) Until one day (Pause) his wife canned her!

You should have been at this Board meeting. (Long pause) There wasn't enough marbles in the room to get up a game!

FAMILY

The best part of his family tree is under ground!

His family tree could use a lot of trimming!

Charlie, of course, is a great family man. (Long pause) But then so was Charles Manson!

My mother is nearly 70. Her whole life she told us she only slept with one guy! (Long pause) She won't tell us who!

When Charlie's grandmother was 60, she started walking 5 miles every day. Today she is 92. (Long pause) They have no idea where the hell she is!

Ralph's family has great genes. Everyone lives forever. His Grandmother still doesn't use glasses. (Long pause) Drinks right out of the bottle!

A big evening for his family is sitting around the barn, (Long pause) watching a saddle dry rot!

Happiness is having a large, loving, caring, close-knit family. (Long pause) In another city!

Charlie's grandfather was an old Indian fighter. And, of course, his grandmother, (Long pause) was an old Indian!

Charlie has two sisters who really get along well together. Well, God made them sisters, (Long pause) but Prozac made them friends!

Charlie lent his brother $20.00 and he never saw him again. (Long pause) He said it was the best investment he ever made!

He's like a father to me! (Long pause) Ever since he started fooling around with my mother! (Don Rickles)

My wife and I got into it again. She said she wanted to see her family, so I dropped her off at the zoo! (Long pause) The woman has no sense of humor!

I can say this about Charlie. (Pause) No one in his family suffers from insanity. (Long pause) They all seem to enjoy it!

When I got married I wanted a large family, (Pause) and I got one. (Long pause) My wife's!

When he was a young man, my brother ran away with the circus. (Long pause) The cops made him bring it back!

In his family, (Pause) he's the idol. (Long pause) He's been idle about six years!

What a man. Each week he sends his mother a big package——every week! (Long pause) She washes and irons it and sends it right back! (Jack Carter)

His family had so much money (Pause) his parents got a boy for their dog!

Talk about a rich family. (Long pause) They had Swiss money in an American account!

When his family moved into town, (Pause) they were fired on by the Welcome Wagon!

His parents are in the iron and steel business. (Long pause) His mother irons, and his father steals!

FINANCE

Long range planning in this outfit (Pause) seems to be everything up to Friday afternoon!

When Charlie was young, he thought that money and power would bring him happiness. (Long pause) It did!

He's a C.P.A.! You know, (Long pause) Constant Pain in the Ass!

This is a man who really knows how to handle the cash flow. When he dies, his tombstone will say, "He died on August 15th, (Pause) as of July 1st."

Business is really looking up. We carpeted our bathroom this year. If we do as well next year, (Pause) we're going to carpet the path out to it!

These days, if you can afford the interest rate, (Pause) you don't need the loan!

Money doesn't always buy happiness. A man with 20 million isn't that much happier (Long pause) than a man with 19 million!

Grapes are two dollars a pound. It's ridiculous. (Long pause) One good orgy could break you!

Recession is when the man next door loses his job. Depression is when you lose your job. Panic (Pause) is when your wife loses her job!

Now that I've taught my kid the value of a dollar, (Long pause) he wants more money!

I've been rich and I've been poor. (Long pause) Rich is better!

A Company that survives a recession is like a tea bag. It doesn't really know how good it is (Pause) until it gets into hot water!

Inflation: A process, which allows you to live in a more expensive neighborhood, (Pause) without bothering to move!

The definition of a living wage depends upon whether you are getting it, (Pause) or giving it!

Remember two can live as cheap as one, (Long pause) as long as one is a bird!

For years there's been talk of a housing shortage, but don't you believe it? It's just a vicious rumor (Long pause) started by a bunch of people with no place to live!

He's got a Polish accountant who absconded with the accounts payable!

You can always tell if a person is lying by looking into his eyes. (Put on a pair of sunglasses) And so, I'm here today to deliver this financial report!

I have all the money I'll ever need. (Long pause) If I die on Friday!

Charlie, of course, is an auditor. Auditor. (Long pause) Those are the people who go in after the battle and bayonet the wounded!

Charlie is an economist. As you know, (Long pause) economists have forecast seven out of the last four recessions!

The problem with inflation is, (Pause) it comes at a bad time. (Long pause) Just when prices are high! (Barry Goldwater)

What an investment genius I am. If I had bought Manhattan Island for $24.00 (Long pause) I would have sold it a week later for $26.00!

In Arthur Andersen's accounting offices around the country they have installed a little red box on the wall with a sign that says: In an EMERGENCY, BREAK GLASS. Inside, (Long pause) are two tickets to Switzerland!

There is a difference between the short income tax form and the long form. Basically, if you use the short form, the government gets the money. If you use the long form, (Long pause) your C.P.A. gets the money!

Business is bad. (Pause) You should have been here yesterday. (Long pause) Somebody should have been here yesterday!

FUND RAISING

Charlie is truly a man of vision. He staged a bullfight as a fund-raiser (Long pause) for the Society For The Prevention of Cruelty to Animals!

GAMBLER

Did you hear about the new three million-dollar Arkansas State Lottery? (Long Pause) The winner gets 3 dollars a year for a million years!

He bet me 4 to 1 he could quit gambling any time he wanted!

These games of chance at the supermarket are getting to be ridiculous. My store doesn't have a manager anymore. (Long pause) They have a pit boss!

Charlie was walking down the street wearing only a barrel. A cop asked him if he was a poker player and he said, "No, (Long pause) but I just left a bunch of guys who are!"

GENERAL

Has anybody ever actually seen an airline seat cushion float? (Long pause) If it's such a great flotation device, (Long pause) why don't you see them at the beach?

The first thing I learned in scouting was if you want to start a fire, you have to have two sticks! (Long pause) And one of them has to be a match!

Charlie's a Realtor. Realtor. (Pause) That's someone who couldn't make it as a used car salesman!

We had some milk really go bad on us the other day. I mean really bad! The carton had a picture (Long pause) of the Lindbergh baby on it!

I really enjoy the south. I love Dixie! (Long pause) Well, I've used their cups for years!

He's really into boating. Boating. That's a hole in the water surrounded by wood (Pause) into which one pours money!

Tonight, Charlie will answer that age-old question. If a light sleeper can sleep with a light on, (Pause) can a hard sleeper, (Pause) sleep with the window open? (Jerry Lewis)

This is a man who went to the ballet and saw all the girls on their toes. Do you know what he said? (Long pause) Why don't they get taller girls? (Paul Lind)

It's really warm in here tonight. I'm perspiring. (Pause) My god, I'm getting malaria! (Don Rickles)

Charlie told me, "Cheer up, things could get worse!" (Pause) So I cheered up and sure enough, (Pause) things got worse!

Charlie just remember, if you did everything right, (Pause) you'd be a woman!

Being run out of town on a rail isn't very pleasant. Actually, if it wasn't for the honor of the thing, (Pause) I'd just as soon not!

Now despite what you might think, Detroit (or any town you choose) is not the end of the world. (Long pause) But you can see the end of the world from Detroit!

Smoking is now considered to be 4 times worse than they originally said it would be. (Long pause) And they originally said it would kill you!

Some girls think those new bathing suits are indecent. (Long pause) Other girls (Pause) have good figures!

He's done a good deal for a lot of people. He's kept a flock of (Pause) detectives, bill collectors, and Treasury men working regularly!

Miami is a very sophisticated town. (Pause) And we were lucky enough to run into him down there!

For it was Maid Marian who said, (Long pause) "I will not live in a house with a Little John!"

Do you know the difference between genius and stupidity? (Long pause) Genius has limits!

Charlie is quite an author. His first book is in its sixth printing! (Pause) Actually, if he could print faster he would be further along!

I do my exercise really early in the morning. Well, I have to do it that way, (Pause) before my brain can figure out what's going on!

I always thought a flashlight was just a tube to hold dead batteries!

Charlie is a very compassionate guy. He firmly believes in forgiving his enemies, (Long pause) after they've been killed!

You ought to see this guy's house. Talk about big! I went through 3 red lights just to get there! (Long pause) And that was just in the driveway! (Nippsy Russell)

Mama, I have da biggest feet in da third grade. Is dat becoss I'm Norwegian? She said, "No, (Pause) it's because you're nineteen!"

This is the only town I've ever been in that has a sign that reads, (Pause) "Last Massage Parlor Before Freeway!"

That Mick Jagger, he could French kiss a moose. He's got childbearing lips! (Joan Rivers)

Help a man who is in trouble and he will remember you, (Long pause) when he is in trouble again! (Nippsy Russell)

On employment applications where it says, "Whom shall we notify in case of an emergency?" (Pause) I put, (Pause) "Doctor!" (Pause) I mean what the hell is my wife going to do? (Steven Wright)

A friend of mine has his answering machine on his car phone. The message is, "Hi, I'm home right now (Long pause) so I can't come to the phone. (Long pause) If you leave your name and number, (Long pause) I'll call you when I'm out!" (Steven Wright)

Charlie worked at the dairy so long, (Long pause) he won't even go to a topless bar!

Charlie's in the chemical fertilizer business. (Long pause) He has a whole herd (Pause) of plastic horses!

Charlie has the only liquor store in the state, (Long pause) that holds a "Back to School" sale!

Charlie's daughter is now going out with a professional man. (Long, long pause) He's a Notary Public!

In Texas, (or any state) they have developed a train that will go 400 miles per hour. (Long pause) Which isn't a bad way to go through Texas!

You can't imagine how bad of a housekeeper this woman is. (Long pause) Last week, (Long pause) Good Housekeeping magazine cancelled her subscription!

Have you seen the new "See Through" dress? That's a dress that isn't all there, (Long pause) for women who are!

The whole country is going to pot. (Long pause) Now the big thing (Pause) is belly dancers!

The whole world is crazy. About 6 months ago two cans of paint got married. Last week she snuggled up to him and said, (Long pause) "I think I'm pigment!"

There is a new book out called "Lord Of The Flies." (Long, long pause) It's about the guy who invented the zipper!

This is a man who followed the proverbial advice, "Build a better mouse trap." And it worked! (Long, long pause) He attracted better mice!

We have a lousy gardener. This morning I heard the crabgrass singing (Long pause) "We shall overcome!"

Michelangelo, the poor man, you talk about depression. Seven years he spent on the scaffold, painting, painting, painting and finally he said to his wife, "What do you think?" She said, (Long pause) (Cup your hand to your mouth and yell) "I said blue!"

I Love summer time. It's when the pools and bikinis (Long pause) are filled to capacity!

Have you ever watched an afternoon soap opera on T. V.? Within a five-minute period, there was an orgy, a half dozen seductions and a drug party. (Long, long pause) And this was at the P. T. A. meeting!

Last month I got a phone bill for $350.00. Can you believe that? Either the bill is wrong, (Long pause) or the dog has learned how to dial!

George Washington was a really smart guy. He had an incredible memory. All over America there are monuments (Long pause) to the memory of George Washington!

He comes from a really healthy town. (Long pause) They had to kill a guy to start the cemetery!

I've got quite a green thumb and I know the first thing you do with a garden is to turn it over. (Long, long pause) Turn it over to someone who knows what the hell they're doing!

What an actor. He's appearing in a remake of the Naked and The Dead. (Long pause) He's playing both parts!

You know you work really hard to keep the wolf from your door. Then your daughter grows up (Long pause) and brings one right into the living room!

My secretary came in the other day and said there was a guy in the lobby looking for a job and he said he used to make his living by sticking his right arm in a lion's mouth. I said, "What's his name?" She said (Long pause) "Lefty!"

GOLF

I play golf in the mid 80s. (Long pause) If it gets much warmer than that, (Pause) I don't play!

I played golf with him the other day and I now know what I'm going to get him for Christmas. (Long pause) A calculator!

This guy's quite a golfer. He's a two-handicap! (Pause) He has a wife who won't let him out (Pause) and a boss who won't let him off!

What a golfer this guy is! I played a new course with him the other day. On the very first tee he missed a hole in one, (Long pause) by only six strokes!

My grandson is a really good golfer! I'll tell you just how good he is! (Pause) He's been offered a scholarship to medical school!

Golf is a wonderful way to spoil a nice walk!

Have you seen this guy play golf? Let me put it this way. He has the only golf cart I've ever seen, (Long pause) that's four-wheel drive!

Charlie will never be a golfer! He hasn't got it! No matter how hard he tries. The other day I said, "Charlie, what kind of clubs do you use?" He said, (Long pause) "Clubs?"

Charlie told me that his doctor told him he couldn't play golf! I said, (Long pause) "He's played with you too!"

My Scottish grandfather quit playing golf about 15 years ago. But he started up again last week! (Long pause) He found his ball!

This is a man who wanted to be a golfer in the worst way. (Long pause) He made it!

I learned one thing about playing golf. Hitting the wrong ball on the fairway is the fastest way I found to make new friends!

The judge asked, "And how exactly did the trouble start?" Charlie said, "Well, she asked me to play a round. (Long pause) I didn't know she was a golfer!"

I watched this guy lose 2 golf balls (Long pause) in the ball washer!

I used to watch a lot of golf on T.V. Then my doctor told me I needed more exercise. (Long pause) So now I watch tennis!

I always thought that the game of golf was created (Pause) so guys like Charlie could dress up like pimps!

Charlie plays golf religiously. Which means if he gets a good shot, (Pause) it's a miracle!

Charlie turned to his caddy and said, "This golf is a funny game!" The caddy said, (Long pause) "It's not supposed to be!"

Charlie turned to his caddy and said, "Do you think I can get there with a 5-iron?" The caddy said, (Pause) "Eventually!"

Charlie turned to his caddy and said, "I've played so poorly all day, and I think I'm going to go drown myself in that lake!" His caddy said, (Long pause) "I don't think you can keep your head down that long!"

Charlie turned to his caddy and said, "Please stop checking your watch all the time caddy. It's distracting!" His caddy said, (Pause) "It isn't a watch, (Long pause) it's a compass!"

When he plays golf, he wears two pair of pants. (Long pause) In case he gets a hole-in-one!

This guy is so used to cheating at golf, that the other day he got a hole-in-one. (Long pause) On his scorecard, (Long pause) he put a zero!

After going through three sets of golf clubs and twelve years of lessons, I'm finally getting some fun out of golf. (Long pause) I quit!

My wife said, "How come you don't play golf with Charlie anymore?" I said, "Would you play with a guy who cheats and moves the ball when you're not looking? (Long, long pause) Well neither will Charlie!"

Charlie was playing golf with his preacher the other day and the good parson in an attempt to reform Charlie said, "I have observed that the best golfers are not addicted to bad language." Charlie said, "What the hell do they have to swear about!"

We were out playing the other day and Charlie said, "I'd move heaven and earth to be able to break 100." The caddy said, "Try heaven, (Long pause) you've already moved most of the earth!

Golf is like taxes. You drive hard to get to the green, (Long pause) and then you wind up in a hole!

The other day after nine holes he had a perfect 36. (Long pause) She dumped him when she saw the wedding ring!

HECKLER RESPONSES

If they ever put a price on your head, (Long pause) take it!

Someday you'll go too far, (Pause) and I hope you stay there!

You take good care of him, lady. Men like him don't grow on trees. (Pause) They usually swing from them!

My sweet, beauty is only skin deep, (Pause) and you are beginning to peel!

Lady, if sheep ever learn to cook, (Pause) you're a goner!

I see the wheel is spinning, but the Hamster's dead!

An intellect rivaled only by garden tools!

Well, the lights are on but no one seems to be home!

My cow died this morning, (Pause) so I don't really need your bull tonight!

My friend, if your funeral takes place while I am in town, I will forego all other forms of entertainment and attend! (Mark Twain)

Lady, you keep it up and I'm going to tell everybody your real age!

Oh, I see some village is being deprived of its idiot!

If his I.Q. were 4 points higher, he'd be a geranium!

Sir, with respect to your last remark, (Long pause) and I hope it was!

(If you're being attacked by someone) I feel like a tree on the Lassie Show!

My friend, I'd like to give you a going away present, (Long pause) but you'll have to do your part!

HUNTING-FISHING

I have a hunting friend who tried to climb through a barbed wire fence with a loaded rifle. (Long, long pause) He is survived by his wife, two kids and a rabbit!

Charlie came in the other day and announced he had shot an elk. I asked him how he knew it was an elk. He said, (Long pause) "By his membership card!"

I didn't know he was so interested in hunting. One day I took him on an Easter egg hunt. (Long pause) He shot three eggs!

Talk about macho. (Pause) This is a man who will get a woman pregnant (Pause) just to kill a rabbit!

55

Charlie and I were going fishing. I called him up the night before to remind him to bring a pole! (Long pause) He brought some guy named Walinski!

But Betty is a fashionable gal. If she did decide to shoot Charlie, (Long pause) she'd wear a hunting outfit!

When Charlie goes on Safari, (Pause) the lions roll up the windows!

I read a really small book today. It was entitled, (Pause) "A Quaker's Guide To Guns And Ammo!"

This is a man who sits on his roof at Christmas (Long pause) hoping to fill his deer tag!

This is a man who has his taxidermist on speed dial!

IMMIGRATION

Today we consider the question: What is the Statue of Liberty doing in New York (Pause), when it's Miami that needs it?

We can trace 90% of the problems in this country, (Pause) back to a lousy immigration policy by the Indians!

INCOME TAX

You want to have some fun? (Pause) Call up the IRS and ask for an audit!

I'll tell you the quick way to figure your gross income for your tax return. It's the figure halfway between (Pause) what your wife tells her friends you make, (Long pause) and what your boss thinks you're worth!

I'll tell you how quick this man is. The IRS called him and told him to come down and bring his records. (Long pause) He brought Sinatra records, and some Nat King Cole records!!!

The IRS agent asked Charlie if this was the first time he had ever been called in for an examination. Charlie asked him how he knew this was his first examination? The guy said, (Long pause) "You really don't have to take off your clothes!"

I hate income tax. (Pause) Every time my ship comes in, (Long pause) the government unloads it!

The new simplified income tax for next year just came out. There are only three lines.
     A.   How much did you make?
     B.   What do you have left?
     C.   (Long pause) Send B!

He's come up with a foolproof way to avoid taxes. (Pause) He doesn't work!

INSURANCE

Being Charlie's age has several notable advantages. The most important of which, (Pause) is that life insurance salesmen no longer bother you!

Charlie is quite an insurance man. He sold me a fire and theft policy. The policy pays off (Long Pause) if I get robbed during a fire!

Charlie just paid his automobile insurance and it's a little ridiculous. (Long pause) He had to sell his car to do it!

INTRODUCTIONS AND OPENINGS

Charlie is the best known and the most distinguished citizen, (Long pause) to ever come from his block!

This man is a sex symbol for women who no longer care! (Milton Berle)

This is the Bert Reynolds of the menopause set!

Well Charlie, you and Helen have had a lot of good years together. (Pause) Either that or you've got a dandy prenuptial agreement!

Earlier someone referred to this dais as distinguished. (Long pause) They all look to me like they made love to Eleanor Roosevelt!

Our next speaker is very articulate. (Long pause) He can bore you on any subject!

Folks, my job is to introduce these people. I don't guarantee them!

Did you enjoy that wonderful chicken dinner tonight? (Pause) Mine tasted like it was beaten to death!

We all got together and drew lots to see who would M.C. the program tonight. (Long pause) I lost!

Well, I'm your M.C. for tonight's program. A responsibility that ranks in importance right up there with being chairman of the N.R.A.'s Hillary Clinton for President Committee!

It's not my job to come out here tonight and bore you. (Long pause) But to introduce people who will!

I've seen a lot of speakers who don't need an introduction! (Long pause) Here's a guy who doesn't deserve one!

I have been asked to appear here tonight and say a couple of words about our guest of honor. (Long pause) Cheap and horny come to mind!

I know Charlie pretty well and I know he won't bore you with a long speech. (Long pause) He can bore you with a short speech!

You can say that Charlie is a modest man. (Long pause) With good reason you can say that!

I'm proud to be here tonight to pay honor to Charlie. I like the guy! (Long pause) I have no taste, but I like him!

We talked a good deal about what kind of gift to get you tonight Charlie. What do you get a guy who has everything? (Long pause) I mean besides penicillin!

Our next roaster is not someone you would call a professional speaker. (Pause) For reasons that will soon become apparent!

In my book he's a truly great man. (Long pause) But then I only do fiction!

This man is my best friend. (Long pause) Which should give you an idea of how lousy my social life has been!

(If you have had several speakers go ahead of you) You know I could stand up here tonight and be really funny. (Long pause) But that would change the entire format of the evening!

Our guest of honor has been wonderful tonight, a really good sport. (Long pause) Either that or he has no idea what's going on around him!

I am delighted to get up and talk. I have been sitting between Bill and Henry all night explaining every joke to them and I'm sick of it! (Joey Bishop)

That was great Charlie. You are a man of many talents. (Long pause) None of which were obvious tonight!

Charlie is our M.C. all right, (Pause) a Mental Case!

I am delighted tonight (Long pause) to be here at the home!

(If the audience is slow reacting to your joke) Folks if you're taking your medication, you'll get these 3-5 times faster!

You've got as much chance of coming out of this evening unscathed, (Long pause) as the Pope does of being convicted of wife beating!

And now, (Pause) I would like to introduce the darling of the menopause set!

Thank you for that well meant (Pause) but rather pedestrian introduction! (Orson Wells)

I will direct my remarks to Charlie (Pause) who is being honored here tonight, (Long pause) for reasons that elude me! (Orson Wells)

This is one of the greatest nights this city's ever had. On this occasion, and in your honor, (Pause) every pizza parlor in the city, (bowling alley) has been closed!

(To use while people are laughing about a joke in which you slammed Charlie). Look at your watch and yell off to the side, "Is the car warmed up?"

(Look at Charlie and say), Charlie, if this is too fast for you, just raise your hand and I'll try to slow it down!

Of all the introductions I've had, (Long pause) that was the most recent! (Milton Berle)

Our next speaker is a man who has risen to every occasion. His colleagues are impressed. His competitors are amazed, (Long pause) and his wife is delighted!

Now I would like to introduce (Pause) Yogi Bear's speech teacher!

Not bad for a guy who thinks Taco Bell is the Mexican phone company!

(To use to introduce the second male speaker in a row) And now, another pretty face!

This show is full of surprises isn't it? (Long pause) I wish to hell it were full of talent!

(After you have been introduced) "That was wonderful, Charlie." (Pause) I wish I was one of those people who didn't need an introduction!"

I won't spend this whole evening talking about the shortcomings of our guest of honor, (Long pause) when it will take me only two minutes to talk about his accomplishments!

He has appeared before both Houses of Congress and hundreds of organizations from coast to coast. (Long pause) But never twice!

Most of you probably didn't know that Betty's middle name was Joan. She was named after Joan of Arc. (Long pause) Not long after her either!

I had to cancel an appointment with my Proctologist just to be here! (Long pause) And I think I made a mistake!

At every banquet I have ever attended, some idiot is selected to introduce people everyone already knows. Tonight, (Long pause) I am the designated idiot!

(To use after a dull speaker has sat down.) Everybody doesn't have to be funny all the time. (Long pause) Charlie proved that tonight!

You notice in my initial remarks how frequently I mention Charlie's name. (Long pause) That's so we can identify the body later!

This is a swell party. (Pause) I've never been to a Bar Mitzvah before!

This is just like old times, Charlie (Pause) you sitting on your duff, (Pause) me working!

Ladies and Gentlemen, I'm here tonight to honor Charlie Jones. (Long pause) Which gives you some indication as to how my career has been going lately!

My job tonight is to be so dull that the succeeding speakers will look brilliant by contrast. Well, I've looked over the list of speakers. (Long pause) I don't think I can do it!

Relax Charlie; (Pause) you look like Bill Clinton's defense lawyer!

Relax Charlie; (Pause) you look like Evil Knievel's insurance man!

You know, Charlie, in planning for this evening, I feel like a mosquito in a nudist camp. (Long pause) I hardly know where to begin!

In your honor Charlie, we have invited the most influential and important people in the city to be here tonight. (Long pause) Unfortunately, (Pause) none of them could make it!

Relax Charlie. You have as much chance of coming out of this evening unscathed, (Long pause) as Dolly Parton does of drowning!!!!

The only thing that would have kept me away from an affair as important as this (Long pause) would have been a Klu-Klux-Clan dinner!

This is a pretty grim audience. You people are looking at me (Pause) like I was your daughter's first date!

Tonight I feel like ZaZa Gabor's 12th husband on his honeymoon. I know what I'm supposed to do. (Long pause) But how do you make it interesting?

As you know, this is a $1,000-a-plate dinner. I don't know who came up with that price, (Pause) but I think it was my dentist!

It is a little intimidating to be here tonight. As I look around at this dais, (Long pause) I'm the only one up here I haven't heard of!

It's not only an honor to be here tonight, (Pause) but also a damn inconvenience!

Welcome to the Henry Kissinger Comedy Hour!

That was great Charlie. Those remedial reading classes really helped!

That was an interesting presentation Charlie. (Pause) My mind needed a rest!

The night is young! (Pause) But Charlie isn't, so we better move this thing along!

(If you appear later in the program) I hope I don't repeat anything that's been said here tonight, (Long pause) but I fell asleep just after this thing started! (Bob Newhart)

Charlie, this room isn't big enough to hold all your friends, (Long pause) so we invited your enemies! (Long, long pause) And I see they all came! (Dean Martin)

I said to him, "Why did you come here tonight half drunk?" He said, (Pause) "I ran out of money!"

There are people who go through their whole lives and never have a night like this. (Pause) They're called, (Pause) "The lucky ones!" (Lucille Ball)

That was great Charlie. (Long Pause) You have all the comedy timing of the Cuban invasion! (Johnny Carson)

Good evening friends and admirers of Charlie Jones. (Long pause) And any other minority groups that are here tonight!

When we announced that this man would be our honoree (Pause) the big names started rolling in. (Long pause) They called him every name in the book!

My fantasy was to kiss Helen Jones, (A member of the dais) (Long pause) until I met her tonight!

People say to me, why are we honoring Charlie tonight? (Long pause) Well I can tell you, (Long pause) I have no idea!

This dais looks like a live wax museum! (Milton Berle)

The government presented him with a special cup. (Long pause) which he's wearing tonight!

Now I would like to say something nice about Charlie. (Long, long pause) Anybody know anything nice to say?

There are more losers at this dais (Pause) than in Las Vegas! (Milton Berle)

You look like a friendly crowd tonight (Long pause) (Point at someone) except for you!

Looking over this dais reminds me of an old movie. (Long pause) The Dirty Dozen! (Ernest Borgnoine)

(When you're the first speaker) Charlie, you are one of the finest people in America. (Long pause) That's the first lie you're going to hear tonight!

Many times I am called upon to talk about someone I don't know. (Long pause) As is the case tonight! (Ted Knight)

(Turning toward the guest of honor) I'm surprised to see you here tonight. (Long pause) They told me it would be somebody important!

Tonight we honor an important man. He is the big gear that drives the machine! (Pause) The big nut behind the wheel! (Ted Knight)

I see we have a mason in the audience tonight. (Point at someone in the back) Thanks for coming! (Long pause). My wife buys your jars!

All of his pals couldn't be here tonight. (Pause). Half of them couldn't find time. (Long pause) The other half are doing it! (Milton Berle)

When I first met Charlie, I vowed to follow this great man's career. (Long pause) Just as soon as he begins one, I'm going to follow it!

(Look out over the audience for a minute) This bunch looks like the birth control clinic at Sun City!

Later on in the program we're going to have a female vocalist with three pretty exciting numbers! (Long pause) 36 - 22 - 36!

And so my friends, I ask you to take your glass, rise to your feet, (Wait until everyone is on their feet) and then (Long, long pause) see if you're sitting on the rest of my speech. (Pause) I can't find it anywhere!

Now I know why they call Charlie the toastmaster. (Pause) Toast. (Pause) That's a square (Pause) with a lot of crust!

I want to tell you how thrilled I am to be here at this audition! (Joey Bishop)

Our honoree is a graduate of Holy Cross University. You've heard about the rambling wreck from Georgia Tech, well tonight (Long pause) we have the total loss from Holy Cross!

What a great M. C. Charlie is. Tonight he's getting three bills for his appearance. (Long pause) Two fives and a ten!

It's wonderful to see all these smiling faces here tonight. The big shots, (Pause) the little shots, (Pause) and those who have come in from the bar. (Long pause) The half-shots!

Today I want to address the number one issue on the minds of everyone in this room. (Long pause) No, this will not be a long speech!

I really enjoy coming up here to talk to you folks because my wife comes along and does all the driving. (Long pause) All I have to do is sit there (Pause) and hold the wheel!

The last speech I heard Charlie give was much like a Texas steer, (pointing) a point here and a point (pointing) there, (Long pause) and a lot of bull in between!

Thank you for inviting me to a return-speaking engagement. (Long, long pause) I was here 28 years ago!

What a great introduction. (Long pause) I can hardly wait to hear what I'm going to say myself!

Charlie was 'Man of the Year' in 1998! (Long pause) That shows you what kind of a year 1998 was!

As I prepared for this evening I said to myself what kind of contribution could I possibly make tonight competing with this group of talented personalities. (Long pause) All I have to offer is (Long pause) a good deal of wit (Pause) and good taste!

It's wonderful to be here tonight (Long pause) on this never to be remembered evening! (Red Buttons)

I'm sorry to announce that we have two disappointments tonight. First Robert Redford couldn't make it tonight. And second, (Long pause) Charlie Jones (Your speaker) could!

It's nice to be here (Long pause) at this marathon for stuttering! (Jack Carter)

This man needs no introduction. (Long pause) What he needs is a conclusion!

Thank you for that fine introduction. (Pause) I'm always amazed what people will say about you (Long pause) when they're not under oath!

(If the microphone is too short) Who were you expecting, (Long pause) Toulouse Letrec?

This has been an all beef dinner. We've had milk from the cow, (Pause) meat from the steer, (Long pause) and now we're going to get the bull!

(Introducing a member of a family business) You know our speaker started in the mailroom of this company almost 15 years ago. And a few short months later (Long pause) someone took a liking to him. (Long pause) His father!

Sex, (Pause) wild adult parties, (Pause) and one million in cash. (Long, long pause) Now that I have your attention (Pause) I'd like to talk about my subject tonight!

Have you ever heard this guy speak before? (Long pause) He couldn't get a standing ovation (Pause) if he closed with the Star Spangled Banner!

My goodness, (Pause) what a lavish introduction. I wasn't sure (Long pause) if I was eight feet tall, (Pause) or six foot under!

(To an audience of experts) You know giving this talk to this audience tonight (Long pause) is like giving a talk on flood control to Noah!

Isn't the human brain a wonderful thing? It never stops working for you from the moment you're born (Long pause) until you stand up to make a speech!

Thank you for that flowery introduction. (Long pause) You're a much bigger liar than I thought!

Thank you for that flowery introduction. (Long pause) I feel like a pancake that has just had syrup poured on it!

I am delighted to introduce a man who is well known for his sporting skills. He has bowled for years and has never (Long pause) lost a ball!

The experiences our next guest has had left him speechless. (Long pause) However, he has completely recovered from that condition and is prepared to talk to us today!

(Before you begin your talk, close your eyes and tilt your head toward the sky) Lord, fill my mouth with worthwhile stuff (Pause) and nudge me when I've said enough!

Good job Charlie. (Long pause) That was about as funny as a bee in a nudist camp!

Relax Charlie. (Long pause) You look like a centipede with athlete's foot!

This is a man who was born in his city (Long pause) at the request of our city!

I was warmed by your comments tonight. (Long pause) Actually, I was burned up!

I thought that introduction was very clever and creative. (Pause) I'll call my attorney tomorrow and see if he agrees with me!

INTROVERTED-QUIET PERSON

This guy's idea of getting a girl in trouble (Pause) is bringing her home after 9:30! (Dean Martin)

What an exciting life this man has. He had us over to his house last week and we spent the entire evening looking at slides from his recent trip, (Long pause) to Bakersfield!

His idea of a big evening is going down to the health store. (Pause) He'll have a couple of shots of carrot juice, and watch the lettuce wilt!

His life is so dull, (Long pause) he looks forward to dental appointments!

This is the only man in America with a 20-year subscription to Reader's Digest!

This is the type of man who goes to the massage parlor (Long pause) for a massage!

This guy (or evening) is about as exciting as watching the Waltons train their pet rock!

(For a real quiet, laid back person) (Point at Charlie) Look at him, a bundle of nerves. (Pause) I took his pulse earlier tonight, I thought he was dead!

This evening is the most excitement that Charlie has seen (Pause) since his sister came home at three in the morning with a Gideon Bible under her arm!

Talk about shy. His wife made him play spin-the-bottle to get him to kiss her on their honeymoon! (Janet Paine)

This guy is so formal. I'd be willing to pay $10.00 to see him with his clothes off! (Pause) I'd even pay $1.00 to see him with his tie off!

Talk about a square. (Long pause) He thinks pot is Tupperware!

This guy is so thoughtful of his neighbors. He holds his New Years Eve party at 2:30 in the afternoon (Long pause) in July! (Lucille Ball)

This is a man who gives new meaning to the word, (Pause) "Valium!"

You talk about being shy and introverted. For years he would only date pregnant women!

His house is so quiet, (Pause) the city made it a hospital zone!

This is a man who gets about as much attention, (Long pause) as the English subtitles on a French porno flick!

But Charlie is a very sensitive guy. Why this past Valentines Day, he held the door open (Long pause) when his wife left to go on her paper route!

What a sensitive man this guy is. Even when he gardens, (Long pause) he has a special nursery for unmarried mums!

This guy could read the Bible in a nudist camp!

ITALIAN

He came from a small town. (Pause) We're talking small. (Long pause) The head of the Mafia was a Filipino!

He thinks Dom Perignon (Pause) is a mafia leader!

I make it a rule never to tell Italian jokes! Do you know what's black and blue and sinks in water? (Long pause) A guy who tells Italian jokes!

I really feel bad. At the fight I punched some Italian in the nose (Pause) and I broke his finger in 3 places!

JEWISH

Charlie is loaded with charisma. Charisma, (Pause) that's a Jewish word for horny!

Do you know the difference between Jewish women and Protestant women? (Long pause) Protestant women have fake jewelry and real orgasms!

We have a really nice Jewish couple next door. The poor woman is really going through it. What a dilemma! They have a gay son (Long pause) who's dating a doctor!

They made this crazy Jew the man of the year! Can you believe that! (Long Pause) I wouldn't vote for him to be Jew of the block!

I ran into Abe in the meat market the other day. I've never seen such frustration. (Long pause) Ham at half price!

Charlie wasn't always Jewish! He went swimming one day (Pause) and ran into a swordfish!

I asked my Jewish friend if there was a really good Jewish wine. He said, the one he hears the most is, (Long pause) (Raise your voice) "I want to go out to dinner tonight!"

I said to my partner, Isador. I said, "Izzy, what do you think of the Taft Hartley bill?" He said, "To hell with it, pay it!"

Charlie told me that a Jewish American princess idea of natural childbirth (Pause) is no make up!

If a Jewish American princess has a waterbed it carries a nickname. (Long pause) "The Dead Sea!"

How do you know if a Jewish American Princess has an orgasm? (Pause) She drops her nail file!

They named a Jewish holiday after his sex life. (Long pause) "Pass Over!"

Abe's wife found a way to keep the kitchen spotless. (Long pause) They eat out!

On their 20th anniversary, Abe's wife insisted he take her some place she had never been. (Long pause) So he took her to the kitchen!

You know it's easy to tell if a Jewish girl is a nymphomaniac. (Long pause) She'll have sex on the same day she has her hair done!

Bar mitzvah. That's when a Jewish boy reaches the age of 13, (Long pause) for those of you from Utah!

There is a new Jewish-American princess horror movie out. (Long pause) It's called, "Debbie Does Dishes!"

The greatest pride in a Jewish home, is to have a son, whose a doctor. Unless he's a little retarded—a lawyer. (Long pause) If his mind doesn't work at all—an accountant! (Jackie Mason)

LADIES MAN

Charlie's ready for marriage. Well, he's had his ears pierced. (Pause) I mean this man has already bought jewelry and experienced pain!

A girl phoned me and said, "Come on over, there's nobody home!" I went over. (Long pause) Nobody was home! (Rodney Dangerfield)

Old Charlie here was quite a rascal. He got his first girlfriend a set of wheels. Then he told her if she cooperated, (Long pause) he'd steal the rest of the car!

I know he's a real farm boy! Last night I saw him at the bar (Pause) with a couple of pigs! (Dean Martin)

Charlie is very strict about the rules in his home. (Long pause) No man can smoke in his house. (Long pause) On the other hand if he has a woman over, she can barbecue a goat in the living room and it's okay!!

I mean what do you give to a ladies man who has everything? (Long pause) I mean besides penicillin!

This is some town. Last night a woman pounded on Charlie's door for 45 minutes. (Long pause) So he let her out!

He is a very social animal. He is constantly inviting women up to his apartment for a scotch and sofa!

What a lover this guy is. You should see him kiss. I haven't seen lip movement like this (Pause) since I gave my dog a sticky tootsie roll! (Phyllis Diller)

This is a man who likes to take pornographic film home and run it backward. (Pause) He likes to see people get dressed and leave! (Nippsy Russell)

When this man goes to Las Vegas, a lot of people gain financially. (Long pause) You never met a finer group of girls! (Foster Brooks)

What makes men chase women they have no intention of marrying? (Long pause) It must be the same urge that makes dogs chase cars they have no intention of driving!

He had his back broken in an air accident. (Long pause) The girl's husband flew in unexpectedly and broke his back.

Have you seen this guy's girlfriend? For Christmas he gave her two silver bowls. (Pause) One was engraved FOOD, the other WATER!

Talk about a ladies man. He goes to England, France and Germany. (Long pause) I can't tell you how many times I found him a broad! (Charlie Callas)

I recently asked him, I said, "Charlie, do you smoke after sex?" He said, (Pause) "I've never looked!"

He's a 3 pack a day man. (Long pause) And that's a lot of condoms!

He has such a bad reputation with the ladies. He joined a key club. (Long pause) They changed all the locks!

The guy has no social skills. The other day this girl at the table next to him leans over, gives him a smile and says, "Will you join me?" He looks at her and says, (Long pause) "Why, (Pause) are you coming apart?"

Charlie met this really pushy girl at a cocktail party. He handed her a plate of hors d'oeuvres and he said, "Excuse me miss, but do you like nuts? She said, (Long pause) "Is this a proposal?"

What an animal this guy is with the ladies. He had to call Triple A the other night and I would have loved to have been there to hear him explain to the driver, (Long pause) how his date got her foot caught in the window!

To him, (Pause) love is just a passing fanny!

He's the kind of guy who goes out with a sweater girl (Long pause) and tries to pull the wool over her eyes!

I'm a little concerned that the girl Charlie is going out with is a little young. Yesterday he asked me, (Long pause) "What wine goes with peanut butter?"

For it was Charlie who said, "Just give me my golf, (Pause) the great outdoors, (Pause) and a beautiful girl. (Long, long pause) And you can keep my golf and the great outdoors!"

When he was in Europe he picked up a little Italian. (Long pause) The only English word she could say was, "No!"

He met her in a revolving door. (Long pause) They've been going around together ever since!

It doesn't bother him that girls kiss and tell. (Long pause) He needs the advertising!

His last girlfriend just left him and he's been drinking for five days. (Long, long pause) That's a long time to celebrate!

I nicknamed Charlie's last girlfriend "Baseball." (Long pause) She wouldn't play without a diamond!

LAWYERS

I worry a lot about our jury system. (Pause) Let's face it. Do you want to be judged by 12 people who aren't smart enough to get out of jury duty?

Charlie is truly a distinguished lawyer. He is a master at creating confusion. Last week he had a trial, (Pause) and the jury convicted the judge!

It's been hard working with my lawyer. Particularly recently. I mean every time you start accomplishing something the guard says, (Long pause) "Visiting hours are over!"

He's a wonderful lawyer. He handled his own divorce, (Long pause) and got custody of his wife's parents!

Charlie's a lawyer. (Pause) Lawyer, that's a Jewish boy who can't stand the sight of blood!

My lawyer took the case on a contingency. (Pause) Contingency. That's an old gold mining term. (Pause) It means he gets the gold and you get the shaft!

"Who is the best lawyer in town?" "Charlie Jones when he's sober." "And who is the second-best lawyer in town?" "Charlie Jones when he is drunk!"

He's a wonderful lawyer, so tenacious. One of his clients was hanged but even then he didn't give up. (Long pause) He sued for whiplash!

I shouldn't complain. I once had a lawyer who was so clumsy. I remember he threw himself on the mercy of the court, (Long pause) and missed!

It has been said that Charlie was the best attorney in the country. (Long pause) Unfortunately, he moved to the City and things really went down hill!

He borrowed $2,000 from his father so he could study law. When he got out of law school, his very first case, (Long pause), was when his father sued him for $2,000!

What is it that a duck can't do, a flamingo can do and a lawyer should do? (Long pause) Stick his bill up his butt!

My lawyer loves his work so much, (Pause) that he named his daughter Sue!

Did you hear about the terrorists who took a whole courtroom full of lawyers hostage? (Long pause) They threatened to release one every hour until their demands were met!

I asked Charlie if his attorney was a criminal attorney. He said, (Long pause) "We think so, (Pause) but we can't prove it!"

It's not important if your lawyer knows the law. (Long pause) It's more important that he knows the judge!

What a lawyer this guy is. I got a traffic ticket, he took it to court and got it changed, (Long pause) to second-degree manslaughter!

My attorney is a bachelor and he's so horny. Last week in court he got carried away and said, "I would like to throw myself on the mercy of the court, (Long pause) not to mention the redhead in the fifth row!"

The Judge asked him, "Are you the defendant in this case?" He said, (Pause) "No sir, (Long pause) I'm the guy who stole the car!"

MARRIAGE

I never doubted the existence of God. (Long, long pause) Until I had been married about six years!

Charlie claims that he's a man who has never gone to bed with an ugly woman. (Pause) He freely admits that he's woken up with a lot of ugly women!

If he was the best man, (Long pause) the maid of honor must have been a bulldog!

Charlie's wife thinks that summer cottages were created for people who like to wash floors in a bathing suit!

In a marriage, the easiest way to get into trouble, (Long pause) is to be right at the wrong time!

May this lovely couple have as much fun and happiness as we have had, (Long pause) on a couple of occasions! (Henny Youngman)

I told Betty that sometimes her husband was a pain in the neck. (Pause) She said her opinion of him was much lower than that!

My brother's wife told me that he brought a little magic into their marriage. (Long pause) He disappeared!

You guys may think that the three little words your wife wants to hear the most is, "I love you." (Pause) Try, (Pause) "I'll fix it!"

Have you ever noticed that the guy your wife almost married (Pause) is always the fastest success story in town!

I met my wife in one of those singles bars. (Long pause) I wish she'd have stayed home with the kids!

Last week I received six invitations to go out for dinner. (Long pause) All from my wife!

Your wife isn't going to be real happy with you tonight Charlie. (Pause) The old electric blanket will be set for headache!

My ex-wife is a great housekeeper! She really is! (Long pause) Six marriages, (Pause) six houses!

Have you ever noticed? Betty does bird imitations! (Long pause) She watches Charlie like a hawk!

I learned a lesson early in my marriage. Never fight with your wife when she's tired. (Long pause) Or when she's rested!

Since he's been married, Charlie quit using scope! No need to worry about that any more! (Pause) He never gets a chance to open his month!

I don't know how many times she's been married. (Long pause) But she has rice marks on her face!

Well, I have to say you do make a wonderful couple. (Long pause) Except for him!

Betty was looking for a really good man before she ran into Charlie. Even though they married, (Pause) she's never abandoned the search!

I'll say this about Charlie and Betty. They're not what you would call a decisive couple. (Pause) Their first kid was 8 before they named him!

I asked him. I said, "Charlie, what did you do before you were married?" He said, (Long pause) "Anything I wanted to!"

He's a man who gives his wife something to live for. (Long pause) A divorce!

When they were first married, they practiced the rhythm method. Until one day she had enough, (Long pause) and told him to get that drummer out of the bedroom!

My wife is a perfect angel! (Long pause) Always up in the air and harping about something!

My wife would have been with us tonight. (Pause) But unfortunately she went swimming in our pool today with her jewelry on and drowned! (Don Rickles)

Now, of course, he's turned into a suburban husband. Suburban husband. (Long pause) That's a gardener with sex privileges!

There was a rumor going around that Betty married him for his money. And if that's true, (Long pause) she's earned every nickel of it!

Charlie's wife went to the doctor. She said, "Doctor, I have a small embarrassing wart." The doctor said, "Divorce him!"

Charlie's been in love with the same woman for 20 years. (Or, however long he's been married.) (Long pause) If Betty (His wife) finds out she'll kill him!

But Charlie turned out to be a model husband. (Long pause) Unfortunately he wasn't a working model!

I asked Betty, I said, "Does Charlie exercise?" She said, "Oh yes, (Long pause) last week he was out four nights running!"

A man can usually tell what kind of a time he's having at a party, (Long pause) when he looks at his wife's face!

"My dad can beat up your dad." (Pause) "Big deal, (Pause) so can my mother!"

"Tell me, Mrs. Smith," said the marriage counselor, after several sessions, "Did you wake up grouchy this morning?" "No," Betty said, (Pause) "I let him sleep!"

Have you ever heard a Polish marriage proposal? (Long pause) "You're gonna have a what?"

They were married in a bathtub. (Long pause) It was a double ring ceremony!

You know your marriage is in trouble when your spouse orders twin beds. (Long pause) And has them delivered to different cities!

Their marriage is a partnership. (Long pause) He's the silent partner!

She's two-thirds married. (Long pause) She's willing and so is her mother!

Marriage is nature's way of keeping people from fighting with strangers!

Wives are not like fishing buffs. They brag about the ones that got away (Pause) and complain about the one they caught!

What could happen so fast? On the morning after my wedding, (Long pause) I was still trying to unhook her bra!

They had three figures on top of the wedding cake, the bride, the groom, (Long pause) and an obstetrician!

There are a few four-letter words that will shake up every bride. (Pause) Like cook, wash, dust and iron!

Every man needs a wife. (Pause) I mean sometimes things go wrong that you can't blame on the government!

Charlie's first wife ran away with his best friend George. (Pause) Of course George wasn't his best friend (Pause) until he ran away with his wife!

His wife tells me he's like a hot water faucet in a cheap hotel. (Long pause) Even when he's turned on nothing happens!

Women have a certain insight that a man doesn't have. I mean if a woman marries someone 20 years younger, (Pause) she knows that she looks like an idiot!

What's the difference between a wife with PMS and a pit bull! (Long pause) Lipstick!

My wife believes in the old adage, never go to bed angry. (Long pause) The woman hasn't slept in eight months!

Marriage is a great institution. (Long pause) For those people ready for an institution!

This man has given his wife something to live for. (Long pause) Revenge!

Charlie tricked Betty into marrying him. (Long pause) He told her she was pregnant!

This is a man who spent his entire honeymoon, (Long pause) looking for the re-set button!

Charlie and Betty are a wonderful couple; Two minds with a single thought. (Long pause) Hers!

Let me give you some advice my friend. If you think marriage is a 50-50 proposition, (Pause) then either mathematics or women confuse you!

Charlie and Betty have been married a long time, primarily because he always remembers her birthday. (Pause) But he can never remember her age!

The other night Charlie loaded the dishwasher. (Long pause) He got his wife drunk!

My wife came down to breakfast the other day wearing a tee shirt that said, "I'm out of Estrogen, and I have a gun!"

Her husband hasn't spoken to her in a year. (Pause) Oh, he's not mad. (Pause) He just can't get a word in! (Nippsy Russell)

How many wives with PMS does it take to change a light bulb? Six. (Pause) Why six? (Raise your voice) It just does, okay!

Charlie's wife made him join the Bridge club. (Long, long pause) He jumps on Tuesday!

You should have been around Charlie and Betty when they were first married. They used to fight so much (Pause) that Bob Hope went over to their house to entertain!

He's been marred 5 times. (Long pause) Now he just leases!

Things aren't going well in our marriage. (Pause) We got into bed the other night and she said, (Long pause) "I'll race you to sleep! (Richard Lewis)

Things aren't going well in our marriage. (Pause) The other night without thinking I yelled, (Raise voice) "Will you keep the knitting down!" (Richard Lewis)

What do you call a woman who knows where her husband is every minute of the day? (Long pause) A widow!

She likes two kinds of men! (Long pause) Foreign and domestic!

Sex? What sex? Last week the state of Alaska (Long pause) named a glacier after my wife!

My wife has discovered an incredible way of keeping all her dishes and pots and pans sparkling clean. (Long pause) She never uses them!

At his first wedding, he had a figure of the bride carved in ice. (Long, long pause) He had no idea that would be a prophecy!

Their marriage started badly. After the first night on their honeymoon, they came down for breakfast (Pause) and asked for separate checks!

For breakfast, he's been eating that new cereal that's great for children. (Long pause) It must work. (Long pause) His wife is pregnant!

I guess I don't pay attention the way I should. My wife came in the other day and said, "Did you miss me while I was gone?" I said, (Long, long pause) "You were gone?"

She has been married so many times, (Long pause) a wedding dress is her native costume!

I'm not sure who married them, (Long pause) but I think it was the Secretary of War!

Charlie is getting suspicious about his wife's activities. She told him that twice as many people drown in bathtubs as do in swimming pools. It must be true, because yesterday he came home (Long pause) and found his wife in the bathtub with a lifeguard!

Charlie proposed to his wife in a restaurant. At the time he ordered a steak with fries, (Long, long pause) and she ordered pickles and a bowl of ice cream!

I really don't like to talk about my wife behind her back. (Long, long pause) It's just safer that way!

I see Charlie brought his wife tonight. I don't know why you would do that Charlie. It's like (Long pause) going on a hunting trip with the game warden!

You have to give Charlie a little space these days because he tends to get cranky. (Long pause) The poor guy is going through 'the change of wife!'

The most difficult thing to explain to your wife is why your son has poison oak, (Pause) why you have poison oak, (Long, long pause) and why your secretary has poison oak!

My wife is a health food nut. She makes me drink tiger milk six times a day. (Long pause) Yesterday I bit the dog!

On their wedding night, they looked like a new house. (Long pause) She was freshly painted (Pause) and he was plastered!

My wife goes to a beauty parlor (Long, long pause) that has a recovery room!

I am firmly convinced that the game of bridge was invented by two married couples (Long pause) that hated each other!

This woman has been married so many times that they quit giving her new licenses. (Long pause) They just punch the old one!

Just remember fellows, no matter how bad things get, in the entire history of the world no woman (Long pause) has ever shot her husband while he was doing the dishes!

An honest woman will only lie about her age, (Long pause) her weight, (Long pause) and how much her husband makes!

My wife told me, "If you really loved me, (Long pause) you would have married someone else!"

Charlie was taking off on a trip to Yellowstone Park and I told him not to forget Old Faithful. (Long pause) He said (Pause) she was coming with him!

Nobody can teach my wife to swim. Nobody! (Long pause) She can't keep her mouth shut that long!

He came home late for dinner the other night (Pause) but she still gave him two kinds of meat. (Long pause) Hot tongue and cold shoulder!

I'm not going to say that my wife lied about her age. (Long pause) But if she were as young as she said she is, (Pause) the best man at our wedding, (Long pause) would have been a cop!

I leaned over to my wife on our honeymoon and I said, (Pause) "I love you terribly!" She said, (Long pause) "I know, (Long pause) and we'll have to work on that!"

Charlie took a message for his wife and left her a note. It said, "Doctor's office called—Your Pabst beer is normal!"

When my wife and I drive together, (Long pause) I get about 2000 words to the gallon!

She was so far along with the pregnancy (Long pause) that at her wedding, (Pause) everyone threw puffed rice!

Charlie goes to Dallas several times a year because he has relations in Dallas. (Long pause) If his wife ever finds out, she'll kill him!

When I first met my wife I think she was ready for marriage. (Long pause) On our first date (Long pause) she wore a wedding dress!

Our wedding was made in heaven. (Long, long pause) But so was thunder and lighting!

My wife is so sentimental. On Easter (Long pause) she gave me a rabbit punch!

We're back to square one. My wife took all the money we were saving for a house and blew it (Long pause) at the super market!

She wanted to marry a famous person or nothing. (Long, long pause) She got her wish!

When we got married we were the same age. (Long pause) I don't know how old she is now!

I can truthfully say my wife is the one responsible for what I am today. (Long pause) Broke!

Charlie thinks he's head of the household. The fact of the matter is (Long pause) he's only chairman of the entertainment committee!

My wife wears a ring that once belonged to a millionaire. (Long pause) Woolworth!

Charlie's sister found out her husband was having an affair with his secretary. (Long pause) She found white out on his shirt collars!

MEDICAL

It's a good thing that God didn't work for Medicare. After making the world in six days, instead of taking the seventh day off, (Long pause) he would have had to fill out all the paper work!

Betty almost didn't pass the state examination to become a nurse. The doctor asked her, "How do you wash genitals?" And she said, (Pause) "The same way you wash Jews!"

He was born by Cesarean Section, but you can't really tell. (Pause) Except when he leaves his office. (Long pause) He always goes out the window!

I got the perfect Christmas present for my doctor. (Long pause) A nurse who knows how to caddy!

It has been said that our guest of honor has the hands of a surgeon and that's true. (Pause) They're always wrapped around a golf club!

How did the female condition we know as PMS come to be called PMS? (Long pause) Because Mad Cow disease was already taken!

This guy is really a good surgeon. He's done several hundred operations. (Long pause) And he has yet to cut himself!

My doctor didn't start out his professional career as a doctor. Actually, he started out as a kidnapper! (Long pause) No one could read his ransom notes so he switched!

My doctor's receptionist called me. She said, "Your check came back!" I said, "We're even! (Pause) So did my lumbago!"

My doctor is so successful that every now and then he can afford to tell a patient there's nothing wrong!

Charlie operated on me last year and I was scared to death. I kept lying there thinking, (Long Pause) "This is the same guy who just a few hours ago (Pause) missed a three inch putt!"

I think it's incredible how HMOs are able to cure poor people faster!

Charlie has an excellent reputation as a physician. I'll tell you just how good he is. (Pause) He can even diagnose problems in patients who don't drink, smoke or overeat!

Do you realize it's cheaper to go to medical school than to have some of these new surgeries they've come up with!

The doctor said to my wife, "You know if he survives the operation, he may have brain damage!" My wife said, (Long pause) "How would we know?"

Charlie of course is a gynecologist. Gynecologist. (Pause) That's a person with long slender fingers and no sense of smell!

Charlie's hospital is now issuing gowns in 3 different sizes. (Pause) Short, (Pause) shorter, (Pause) and don't reach for the cookie jar!

Charlie asked me the other day, "Did the medicine I gave your uncle straighten him out?" I said, "It sure did. (Long pause) They buried him today!"

Charlie tells his patients that jogging is a perfect exercise. Thanks to jogging, for the first time in history, (Pause) people are dropping dead in perfect health!

Please bartender, put two cherries in my manhattan. (Long pause) My doctor told me I should eat more fruit!

You know your HMO is in trouble when the directions to your primary physician's office include, (Pause) take a left when you enter the trailer park!

HMOs are really cutting back. You know they're saving money when your annual breast exam (Pause) is conducted at Hooters!

Betty recently had an operation. It took her doctor a half hour to do the surgery. (Long pause) It will take her 6 months to describe it!

Charlie has a really thriving plastic surgery practice. He's redone most of the women in town. (Long pause) In my day, bringing up the rear was a military expression!

He wears a mask during surgery so his patients can't identify him later. A sign outside his office says 2-4. (Pause) Those are lousy odds!

I had my cholesterol checked the other day. (Long pause) It was higher then my SAT's! (Gary Shandling)

This guy is nuts! The other day he went to his doctor and the doctor said, "Why do you have carrots sticking out of your ears?" And Charlie said, (Long pause) (Raise your voice) "Can you speak up, I have carrots in my ears!"

Charlie is a really good orthopedic surgeon and I thought he was always so religious. Before every surgery, he bows his head, closes his eyes, and I thought he was praying. The other day I leaned over and heard him say, (Long pause) "Foot bone connected to ankle bone, ankle bone connected to the shin bone, shin bone connected to the knee bone!

My doctor told me to take a tranquilizer. I got the generic stuff, (Long pause) Vodka!

I spent three days in Charlie's hospital and now I know why his nurses are called Angels of Mercy. (Long, long pause) You never see them!

Charlie has this patient come in to his office and she says, Every time I have children, I get splitting headaches." Charlie says, "Well Mrs. Jones what does your husband say?" She says, (Long pause) "It's Miss Jones, (Long pause) why do you think I get those splitting headaches!"

Charlie's doctor is a health food nut. He told Charlie that a little honey was good for his health. (Long, long pause) Maybe not!

(To a doctor's wife) Helen finally figured it out. The only way she could get a doctor to make a house call, (Long pause) was to marry one!

When I first put on bifocals I could go down stairs three at a time. (Long pause) Sometimes on purpose!

I just came back from my annual physical. My doctor told me I have so many things wrong with me, (Long pause) he thinks I was made in Detroit!

His doctor had him give up smoking, drinking and women. (Long pause) Now, (Long pause) he's looking for a new doctor!

This is a man who perfected (Long pause) the first hemorrhoid transplant!

MEXICANS

He thinks that Puerto Ricans are Mexicans with jobs!

I know a Mexican family who just went through real tragedy. My friend's brother hung himself, (Long pause) from the rear view mirror!

These guys were sitting on the bus. They were talking to each other in French. I said, "Hey guys, why are you talking French in America! (Long pause) Talk Spanish!"

We stayed with a couple in Mexico! They had two kids. One was Jose! (Pause) The other was Hose B!

MILITARY

During the war, my uncle was a really lucky guy! For 16 months, an Italian couple hid him! (Long pause) Of course, that was in Jersey City!

Charlie's brother met his wife in Canada. He was in the R.O.T.C. program. You know, (Long pause) the "Run Over To Canada" program!

Charlie asked his C.O., "How many successful jumps does a paratrooper have to make before he is ready for combat?" The guy said, (Pause) "All of them!"

He is the only enlisted man in the history of the military to be put on report, (Long pause) for a rusty bow and arrow!

He was the only member of the armed forces ever discharged, (Long pause) for "Bottle Fatigue!"

The military in Poland is something else. I met this Polish Army guy in a bar and he had an orange hat with red plumes, a pink top and green pants with sequins. I said to him, "What branch are you in?" He said, (Long pause) "The Secret Service!"

I think General Custer had a military adviser from Egypt!

I have a cousin who had his first combat experience in Viet Nam. He said he wasn't scared, (Long pause) but he said he passed a lot of guys who were!

I asked this young recruit what he was in civilian life. He said, (Long pause) "Happy!"

The Italian army hired him and he delivered. (Long pause) He developed a parachute (Long pause) that opens on impact!

MOTHER-IN-LAW

My mother-in-law has had so many face lifts, (Pause) that her ears meet!

This is a woman who loves nature. (Long pause) Despite what it did to her!

I was at a family picnic last Fourth of July, and we all wanted to play horseshoes. (Long pause) But my mother-in-law refused to go barefoot!

I don't want to discuss my mother-in-law's figure. (Long pause) But in India she'd be sacred!

The difference between an Italian mother-in-law and an elephant (Long pause) is approximately 50 pounds!

I just came back from the best trip I've ever taken! (Long pause) I took my mother-in-law to the airport!

My mother-in-law's voice sucks! It's really bad. She was in our house the other day and she started singing! (Pause) The canary threw himself at the cat!

The only reason my mother-in-law wasn't on Noah's Ark, (Pause) was that they couldn't find another animal that looked like her!

My mother-in-law was run out of the Gestapo for lack of compassion!

Do you know what the difference is between my mother-in-law and a gorilla? (Long, long pause) Jewelry!

My mother-in-law kept me off balance all the time. (Pause) She would tell my wife, "Never marry for money! (Long pause) Divorce for money!"

I went to my mother-in-law's for Thanksgiving dinner. I took one bite and I said, "Where in God's name did you get this recipe?" She said, (Long pause) "Popular Mechanics!"

My mother-in-law was such a lousy cook, (Long pause) we had to marinate the corn flakes!

Mother-in-laws are like seeds. (Pause) You don't need them but they come with the tomato!

My mother-in-law is not a cook. (Long pause) She's an arsonist!

My mother-in-law's claim to fame is that she was present when they opened Caesar's Palace. (Long pause) Not the one in Las Vegas, (Long pause) the real Caesar's Palace!

They just passed a law prohibiting agitators from crossing state lines. (Long pause) That ought to cut down on visits from my mother-in-law!

I just bought the perfect Christmas gift for my mother-in-law. (Long pause) A one-way bus ticket to Bolivia!

The only time it really pays not to have an opinion (Long pause) is when your mother-in-law and your wife argue!

My mother-in-law drinks a lot of goat's milk. (Long, long pause) Maybe that's why she's always butting in!

Every time my mother-in-law goes with us to the zoo, I have to buy her two tickets. One to get her in (Long pause) and one to get her out!

I'm so depressed. I just found out (Long pause) my mother-in-law has a twin sister!

When my mother-in-law was young, (Long pause) the ultimate weapon was a rock!

At Thanksgiving, my mother-in-law held up a wishbone and asked me if I wanted to make a wish? I said, "I can't, (Long pause) you're already here!"

We went camping with my mother-in-law. In the middle of the night my wife woke me up screaming, "Quick, do something! A bear just went into mother's tent!" I said, "Why should I help? (Long pause) He got himself into this mess, let him get himself out!"

My wife's mother is all right as mother in laws go. (Long pause) But she never does!

Her mouth is like a fire station. (Long pause) Open night and day!

When we were first married, I got along pretty well with my mother-in-law. (Long pause) Because we couldn't afford another baby sitter!

In my mother-in-law's house, a balanced meal is one in which you have a fifty-fifty chance of recovery!

I really hate my mother-in-law. (Pause) Of course without her I wouldn't have my wife. (Long, long pause) That's another reason I hate her!

I should have guessed what kind of cook my wife would be when I met her mother. (Long pause) Her mother had a can opener strapped to her wrist!

This woman gets fan mail from elephants!

This is a woman who never even wears lipstick. (Long pause) She can't keep her mouth closed long enough to put in on!

MOVIES

Charlie has a good buddy. The guy owns a chain of movie houses. Last week his friend died. (Long pause) and was buried at 2:10, 4:20, 6:00 and 8:30!

Disney is coming out with a new movie depicting the problems of a mixed marriage. (Long pause) It stars Smokey the Bear (Long pause) and Flipper!

The Academy Awards are getting a lot more practical. For example, this year's Best Supporting Role (Long pause) went to Maidenform!

I collect old movies. I've got one movie that's so old (Long pause) France was on our side!

I went to see an X-rated movie and the cashier wouldn't sell me a ticket. (Long, long pause) She had a headache!

They're even making X-rated murder movies. (Long pause) The butler did it, (Pause) the gardener did it, (Pause) the handyman did it (Long pause) and so did the cook!

There is so much nudity in moving pictures today. Did you hear that the Oscar for clothing design (Pause) went to a Dermatologist!

MUSICAL

The guy who wrote the song the Hokey-Pokey just died. (Pause) It was a weird funeral. (Long Pause) First they put his left foot in— (T. Gilman)

He always listened to music, French horn records during the day and French horn records at night. (Long pause) He was the horniest guy I ever met! (Ruth Buzzi)

Charlie is a really good singer. He has a very powerful voice. The other day at home he hit a high C (Pause) and spayed the dog! (Milton Berle)

As a young man, Charlie started out on a musical career. He became an orchestra conductor. (Long pause) But he didn't know his brass from his oboe!

Charlie claims he used to be an organist but he gave it up. (Long pause) His monkey died!

Charlie's kid went to Europe to study the violin. (Long pause) The neighbors sent him!

He even snaps his fingers off key!

This new music the kids are coming up with these days is weird. (Long pause) Sounds like a nudist backing into a dog with a cold nose. (Long pause) Set to music!

Composers are coming out of the woodwork. Nowadays if you have half a mind to write a hit, (Long pause) that's about all you need!

When he was in show business he had a three-piece combo. (Long pause) An organ, a cup and a monkey!

This man has music in his soul. (Long pause) Even his shoes squeak!

His friend broke one of the strings on his guitar. (Long pause) But he wouldn't tell him which one!

He can play two tunes. One is Yankee Doodle Dandy. (Long pause) The other one isn't!

He's not very good at singing. (Long pause) But people like to see his Adams apple go up and down!

Have you ever heard him play? When he plays the Star Spangled Banner, (Long pause) people sit down!

He wrote music in bed. (Long, long pause) It's sheet music!

NEWSPAPERS

The teacher asked the class to write in one sentence, what a newspaper does. One small boy said, (Long pause) "It tells you who won and who's been murdered!"

An editor is the man who separates the wheat from the chaff, (Long pause) and throws away the wheat!

Our next speaker is a journalist whose work has appeared (Pause) in every major birdcage in the city!

Charlie writes a daily column. (Long pause) I never miss it. (Pause) I never read it so I never miss it!

Do you belive this newspaper of ours? Did you see the headlines the other day? *Man Hit By Train Critical.* (Pause) Critical? (Long puase) I would have really been pissed!

As a newspaperman, this guy is incredible. Again today he came up with a big scoop. (Long pause) This one was chocolate!

OPTIMIST-PESSIMIST

I ran into a turkey whose a real optimist. Beginning in October, he runs around the barn going, (Long pause) "Baa, Baa!"

A pessimist is a man who believes that all girls are bad. (Pause) An optimist hopes that he is right!

Do you ever get the feeling that an optimist is just someone who isn't paying attention?

Every time he gets in hot water (long pause) he takes a bath!

A pessimist is a reformed optimist!

This guy is really an optimist. (Pause) He heard that turtles live for 200 years so he bought one (Long, long pause) to find out if it was true!

He thinks the girl he's about to marry is better than the one he just divorced!

The guy is the world's leading optimist. He once took his teacher an apple and she gave him a kiss. The next day, (Long pause) he brought her a watermelon!

OUTFITS

On rare occasions when he dresses up, (Pause) he wears brown and white shoes. (Long pause) One of each! (Rose Marie)

That's a lovely dress you're wearing tonight. (Long pause) Is it something from the Rock Hudson collection?"

Nice outfit Charlie. (Pause) I've never seen an orthopedic tuxedo!

Charlie, where did you get that outfit? (Long pause) I didn't think Fruit of the Loom made suits!

His outfit is guareanteed not to shrink, (Pause) unless of course it gets wet!

He used to be the fashion coordinator for the Chinese army!

You're probably wondering why he's wearing an outfit like this tonight. (long pause) It's because his dress didn't come back from the cleaners on time!

I love that outfit, Charlie. (Long pause) Do you think that style will ever come back?

Everything you buy today is imported. Look at this shirt. You know what the washing instructions are? (Pause) "First - find a flat rock!"

Charlie, you look better in cheap clothes than anyone I've ever met!

Look at him! (Pause) He dresses like a pimp on Sesame Street! (Redd Fox)

Why are you dressed like that? (Long puase) Did you lose an election bet?

Look at him! He looks like he got dressed in front of an airplane propeller!

You should see some of the outfits this girl wears. (Long pause) I don't know if she's trying to catch a man (Pausc) or a cold!

PHARMACIST

HMOs are really cutting back. My doctor gave me a prescription for Viagra (Pause) and the pharmacy gave me a popsicle stick and a roll of duct tape!

Charlie is about to open up his new store, but that effort has been delayed. (Long pause) The "Going Out of Business" signs haven't come in yet!

My pharmacist told me that drugs intensify your personality. Particularly (Pause) if you're a jerk to begin with!

This duck walks into a drugstore and he says, "Gimme some Chapstick (Pause) and put it on my bill!"

I don't know how long he's been a pharmacist. But in his day, (Long pause) the miracle drug was Mercurochrome!

POLITICS

Diplomacy is the art of saying "Nice Doggie," (Long pause) until you can find a rock!

This is a politician's rule to live by. If you live in a town that is run by a committee, (Long pause) you better be on the committee!

If you're being run out of town, (Pause) get out in front and make it look like a parade!

A few years ago he ran unopposed, (Long pause) and lost!

He began his career in politics with an identity problem. (Long pause) Nobody knew who the hell he was!

In China, what do they do when the men have erections? (Pause) They vote! Don't get ahead of me like that!

School board members (City Councilmen, etc.) are simply politicians whose deepest secrets (Pause) keep them from running for higher office!

Maybe the drinking age should be eighteen! You can vote if you're eighteen! When you look at whose running today, (Long pause) you have to drink!

I saw a pregnant woman wearing one of Charlie's campaign buttons that said, (Pause) "Charlie's the man!"

People all over the country are talking about legalizing gambling. I thought we already had it. (Pause) It's called Election Day!

He's been involved with the politics so long, he was the first man ever to recognize that Eleanor Roosevelt had great legs!

He's been in politics so long (Long Pause) he even knows how to start a riot. You just walk into the kitchen of any Mexican restaurant and yell, (cup your hand to your mouth) IMMIGRATION!

What's the matter with those politicians? Why don't they give the little man what he really wants? (Long pause) A little woman!

Charlie's campaign folded so fast, (Pause) they named a beach chair after it!

You can't fool all the people all the time (Long pause) but some politicians figure that once every four years is good enough!

I know a girl who joined Charlie's campaign because of a psychological problem. (Long pause) She's afraid of crowds!

Charlie was very active in politics. When his party won, they figured he was too dumb for the police department. (Pause) So they put him on the school board!

You know Democrats are better lovers than Republicans! (Long pause) Ever hear of a good piece of elephant?

Democracy means that anyone can grow up to be President, (Long pause) and anyone who doesn't grow up can be Vice President! (Johnny Carson)

It's good to have Charlie here tonight. He's the only Republican (Democrat) out on bail! (Johnny Carson)

Politicians and diapers have something in common. They should both be changed regularly! (Long pause) And for the same reason!

He's been in politics for 20 years (Or whatever is appropriate) (Long pause) and has never been caught!

Politics is a lot like sex. (Long pause) You don't have to be good at it to enjoy it! (Pat Henry)

One of the interesting things about politics is that one week you're on the cover of Time. (Long pause) Next week, you're doing it!

This is a man who, if you were drowning 20' from shore, (Pause) would throw you a 15' rope! (Pause) Then he would send his press secretary to the three networks to point out that he had met you more than half way! (Mort Saul)

This is a man of action. He recently proposed legislation that would make the United States a member (Long pause) of the International House of Pancakes! (Audrey Meadows)

He's been on the road speaking at one fundraiser after another. (Pause) He's raising money, (Long pause) to buy a snowplow for the city of San Diego!

(To a chubby politician) I think he's a shoe in for his reelection. I can't imagine anyone else who would be able to fill his seat the way he does!

Some politicians are hawks, some are doves. (Long Pause) Personally I don't care as long as we can get rid of some of the turkeys! (Dean Martin)

Here's a guy who started out working for a department store as a window dresser where you have to work with dummies, (Long pause) and of course it was just a short step into politics! (Dean Martin)

Charlie told me to follow in his footsteps. But I couldn't do it! (Long pause) I wanted to win!

Talk about a conservative. Next to him, (Pause) Calvin Coolidge was an acid freak! (Mark Russell)

This has been a hot issue and Charlie received plenty of phone calls about it. (Pause) And he's doing something about it. (Long pause) He's getting an unlisted phone number!

What a politician this guy is. (Pause) He's to public speaking what termites are to an old barn.

In politics you have a group of dynamic leaders, (Pause) then you have some who are just doing the job, (Pause) and then you have some who don't measure up. (Long, long pause) Well Charlie's in there somewhere!

Well I was dumb struck. I don't know how you lost that last election. It must have been bad timing. (Long pause) You happened to have run on the same day as Bill Baker! (His opponent who won) (Foster Brooks)

Future historians will be able to study at the Jimmy Carter Library, the Gerald Ford Library, the Ronald Reagan Library, and (Long pause) the Bill Clinton Adult Bookstore.

Did you hear? Japan has donated 500,000 bottles of Viagra to the U.S. (Long pause) Seems they heard we can't get an election right!!!

Ninety-eight percent of the adults in this country are decent, hardworking, honest Americans. It's the other two percent that gets all the publicity. But then, (Long pause) we elected them! (Lily Tomlin)

Too bad the only people who know how to run the country (Long pause) are busy driving cabs and cutting hair! (George Burns)

I was pulled over in Massachusetts for reckless driving. The judge asked me, "Do you know what the punishment for drunk driving in this state is?" I said, "I don't know, (Long pause) reelection to the Senate?" (Emo Philips)

He has all the qualities of George Washington, Abe Lincoln and Richard Nixon. (Long pause) He has bad teeth, his clothes don't fit and he has to shave three times a day!

You remember they used to have student government day in high school. Kids got to be government officials for a day. (Long, long pause) Charlie was Coroner for a day!

The U.N. is trying to get the whole world to live as one big family. (Long pause) And if it's anything like my family, (Long pause) they made it!

This man has been in Congress for just a few months and he's already come up with a way to save 50 billion dollars. (Long, long pause) Replace Medicare with Christian Science!

A lot of very prominent people in our community got together and ran him for Congress. (Long, long pause) It was the only way we could get him out of town!

In this election, Charlie has been hurt by more polls (Long pause) than a near-sighted dog!

Did you all go to the city council meeting the other night? (Long pause) Well if you were there, you'll understand (Pause) that not all ding-a-lings are on ice cream trucks!

I understand that the Democrats have decided to turn Oklahoma into another Disneyland, (Long pause) and use Texas for the parking lot!

You've all heard about the mice in laboratories all over America getting cancer. Well last week our congressman stepped in and passed a law. It is now illegal (Long pause) to sell cigarettes to mice!

This is a politician who had greatness thrust upon him, (Long, long pause) and he ducked!

The incumbent generally has the edge in an election. And if you don't believe me, (Long, long pause) ask Genghis Khan!

Our speaker tonight is a man of whom the President of the United States once said, (Long pause) "Who?"

He's the type of guy who votes for a bond issue, (Long pause) and then moves out of town!

Well, Charlie almost got elected. That's kind of like (Long pause) almost beating the train to the crossing!

(When the microphone doesn't work) I didn't know Democrats (Republicans) made sound systems!

He started out running for office. (Long pause) Lately, he's been spending most of his time (Pause) running for cover!

They say that Congressman Charlie Jones grows on you. (Long pause) So do warts, (Pause) but I've never sent one to Congress!

This year, I want to see something on the school board I've never seen before. (Long pause) Me!

I worry about our school board. We spend $100,000 on a school bus to haul kids one mile. (Long pause) Then we build a 2 million dollar gym for them to exercise!

The basic difference between Republicans and Democrats is, (Long pause) one is in (Pause) and the other is out!

Finally, the Democrats and Republicans have agreed to share something in common. (Long pause) Our money!

Charlie was campaigning the other day and made a passionate speech. He said, "I see a country where there is no bigotry, (Pause) no prejudice. (Pause) A country with clean air. (Long pause) I see Switzerland!"

This is a compassionate politician. When he heard Watts was burning (Long pause) he sent in a truckload of marshmallows! (Foster Brooks)

He thought Henry Cabot Lodge was a motel! (Foster Brooks)

Although Charlie lost the election, the experts are now saying that if he had run just one day earlier, (Long pause) he would have been a shoe in!

This guy changes sides more often than a windshield wiper!

Some politicians can't tell a lie, others can't tell the truth. (Long pause) Most of them can't tell the difference!

I have a friend who has two sons. One became a politician and the other one (Long pause) didn't amount to anything either!

POOR

I grew up sleeping in the same bed with my two brothers. (Long pause) I never slept alone, (Pause) until I got married! (Joey Bishop)

We were so poor, (Pause) that after every meal my mother had to count the kids!

Our family was so poor that if someone threw the dog a bone, (Pause) he would raise his paw and call for a fair catch!

He came from a poor, (Pause) but poverty stricken family.

They used to send him food from Europe!

He was so poor (Pause) his sister was made in Hong Kong!

He was so poor (Pause) his sister didn't get a sweet sixteen party until she was 28!

In Charlie's day, if he had asked his parents for 50 cents more a month in allowance, (Pause) his parents would have thought he was keeping a woman!

Most poor people live on the wrong side of the track. (Pause) He was so poor that (Pause) he lived ON the tracks! (Dean Martin)

He was so poor, when he was a kid if he hadn't been born a boy, (Long pause) he wouldn't have anything to play with!

We were so poor, (Long pause) the tooth fairy left I.O.U.s!

We had a lot of kids in our family and we were poor. I was 17 before I found out there were other parts of the chicken besides the gravy!

Our house was so small (Long pause) the dog had to wag his tail up and down!

This is a man who never went to college because he was poor. (Long pause) Poor at math, poor at English and poor at history!

POST OFFICE

All the rest of us got out of school and went to work in the real world! Not him! (Long pause) He went to work for the post office!

The post office recently tested 50,000 of their employees for drugs. They found traces of everything known to man. (Long pause) Except speed!

The post office people are doing their best. In fact, yesterday I handed one of them a compliment. (Long pause) He dropped it!

Personally, I've always thought that the post office should be taken over by the Red Cross. (Pause) They're used to handling disasters!

PROMOTION

Well, this new position that Charlie has been given clearly supports the old saying (Pause) that determination, hard work and a desire to succeed, (Long pause) don't always work!

He got this promotion way early, (Pause) very, very early. (Long pause) Years before he deserved it!

This promotion couldn't have happened to a nicer guy! (Long pause) Perhaps a lot more deserving, but none nicer!

PSYCHIATRIST

Charlie has begun using a new form of shock treatment in his practice! (Long pause) He sends his bill in advance!

You know what a psychiatrist is? That's a guy who charges you a lot of money (Pause) to ask you the same questions your wife asked you!

Charlie goes to a psychiatrist. He says, "Doctor, sometimes I feel like a tee pee and sometimes I feel like a wigwam." The doctor says, (Pause) "Your problem is you're too tents!"

I say anyone who goes to a shrink, (Long, long pause) should have his head examined!

As a psychiatrist, Charlie spends day after day listening to men complain about their wives. He is now convinced (Long pause) that the Indian is not the only one who sleeps with a battle-ax by his side!

He's a psychiatrist. You know, (Long pause) a guy who goes to porno movies (Pause) just to watch the audience!

PUT DOWNS

Smile Charlie, you look like a Basset Hound (Pause) who forgot where he buried his bone!

Charlie sent his picture to the Lonely Hearts Club. They sent it back with the note, (Pause) "We're not that lonely!"

Charlie learned that he was an unwanted child. He figured it out one day when his father brought him a new bath toy. (Long pause) A toaster! (Joan Rivers)

If idiots could fly, (Pause) this place would be an airport!

She didn't have time this evening to shave her legs. (Pause) So she put them up in curlers!

Until he was about 30, everyone thought he had a really bad case of acne. Not so, (Pause) he just had a hard time learning to eat with a fork!

When she was small, she was really hyper! (Long Pause) She used to steal hubcaps from moving cars!

We have been friends for over 30 years and he still looks the same! (Long pause). Old! (Jessie White)

Charlie is a little slow. (Pause) He thinks that intercourse has something to do with the state highway system!

He's like one of those old kerosene lamps. (Pause) Not particularly bright, he's regularly turned down, he smokes (Pause) and he goes out every night!

His wife had to have the word "STOP" stenciled on the top rung of his ladder to keep him from getting hurt all the time!

This is a man who gets out of breath playing checkers!

This is a man who thinks Moby Dick is a social disorder! (Pause). He thinks ping-pong balls are some kind of Chinese venereal disease!

When he was in the fourth grade he wasn't like the other kids. (Long pause) Because he was 22!

Charlie's mind works like a trap. I said to him, "Spell Mississippi!" Instantly he said, "The state or the river?"

I'll say this about Charlie. He has more brains in his little finger (Long pause) then he does in his big finger!

It takes him an hour and a half to watch 60 minutes!

This is a woman who thinks Johnny Cash is a pay toilet!

No matter how long I live, I will never forget the first time I met Ralph. (Long pause) But I'll keep trying!

Ralph told me the women in his office couldn't keep their hands off him. (Pause) They all wanted to choke him to death!

This man has more balls than a pool table!

This is a woman who needs to start working out. (Pause) If she ran a bath (Pause), she'd come in second!

This is a man who took steroids (Long pause) just to be on the chess team!

Did you folks watch him eat? (Long pause) He has all the grace and manners of Mike Tyson!

He made a pass at an inflatable doll. (Long pause) Her inflatable boy friend beat him up!

Charlie has got a pretty fair sized ego, but I like the guy! (Pause) Not as much as he does!

This is a man who thinks the Trojan War was fought over condoms!

This is a woman who has so many blind dates (Long pause) they gave her a free dog!

This guy is all class. His idea of a seven-course meal (Pause) is a six-pack and a bag of potato chips!

He has an interesting educational background. He's a graduate, (Pause) of the Don Rickles School of Charm!

Charlie, I can truthfully say that you made me what I am today! (Long pause) Depressed! (Phyllis Diller)

He's the new poster boy for "Tidy Bowl!" (Orson Wells)

Charlie, I wish we had 100 people just like you here in our city. (Long pause) Unfortunately, we have about 10,000!

Everybody doesn't have to be funny all the time. (Long pause) And Charlie proved that tonight!

When he was eight, his father took him aside, (Long pause) and left him there! (Dean Martin)

I'd like to shake your hand, (Pause) but I see it's already shaking.

The last time I saw a face like his (Pause) was on an iodine bottle!

He told me he was a West Pointer. (Pause) He looks more like an Irish Setter to me!

Charlie's jokes are not funny. But, (Long pause) his delivery is terrible!

The last time I saw a mouth like his, (Pause) it had a fishhook in it!

Besides eating and drinking, (Pause) Charlie does have a serious side!

Here's a man who has turned his life around. He used to be miserable and unhappy. (Long pause) Now he's unhappy and miserable!

This is a man who started out life as an unwanted child. (Long pause) Now he's wanted in ten States! (Dean Martin)

This man not only starts things he can't finish, (Pause) he starts things he can't even begin!

Here's a man that goes through life pushing doors, (Pause) marked pull!

He's a man who thinks the world is against him, (Long pause) and he's right!

I'll tell you how smart Charlie is. When they had the black out in New York. He was stranded for 13 hours, (Long pause) on the escalator!

Charlie was born ignorant, (Long pause) and has been loosing ground ever since!

On his last birthday, his whole staff got together and bought him a compass with a mirror on the back. (Long pause) So he can tell who's lost!

The last time he stuck his head out of a basement door, (Long pause) they started a hockey game!

But don't let Charlie fool you. He's brighter than he looks. (Long pause) But then he'd have to be!

This guy couldn't run a lady of the street in an Army camp!

He's a legend in his own mind!

She wanted to turn in her menstrual cycle, (Pause) for a Honda!

I asked him, "Charlie, What's a Grecian Urn?" He said, (Pause) "Oh, about a dollar an hour!"

I said, "What's the capital of Poland?" He said, (Pause) "40 cents!"

It goes back to his childhood. Even then he was weak. You've heard of support stockings? (Long pause) He had a support diaper! (Dean Martin)

This is the man who originated the collect call!

Charlie just returned from the 28th Annual Reunion (Long pause) of the Portuguese Suicide Squad!

He waited years for Dame Fortune to knock on his door. But it was her daughter, (Pause) Miss Fortune, who showed up!

You may have noticed that Charlie looks a little tired tonight. He had some lab work this morning, (Pause) and was up all night studying for his Urine Test!

Charlie is a man who started at the bottom, (Long pause) and stayed there!

He is very class-conscious. (Pause) He has no class and everyone is conscious of it!

This man is the reason for birth control!

His mother saw something in him that no one else saw. (Long pause) She saw that he was nuts!

He was the teacher's pet. (Long pause) She couldn't afford a dog!

Every time I see you, you up my morale. Knowing how you feel about me, (Pause) up yours too!

He thinks Peter Pan is the washbowl in a brothel!

Here's a guy who was seriously hurt dunking for french fries!

She's a homebody. And with a body like hers, (Pause) you have to stay home!

Success didn't spoil old Charlie. No sir, (Pause) he still treats us with the same disrespect he always did!

We ought to put you in a hot tub and watch your duck sink! (Don Rickles)

Old Charlie here considers an intellectual discussion, (Long pause) a review of the plots of Gilligan's Island!

You ought to be in a home!

He was a bottle fed baby. (Long pause) Even his mother didn't trust him! (Pat Henry)

This is a man who put his grandmother's bedpan in the freezer!

His wife told me that living with him makes everyday seem like Thanksgiving! (Long pause) That's what she gets for marrying a turkey!

This is a man who knows where it's at! (Pause) Why he doesn't go and get it, I don't know! (Dean Martin)

I can say this! Charlie's parents were great practical jokers. Look at him! (Long pause) His mother moved to Mexico and changed her name!

Charlie's career keeps right on growing. (Pause) He's just been named the national spokesman for Prozac!

This is a man who should not be allowed to breed!

Look at him! (Pause) His sole purpose in life is to serve as a warning to others!

This is the only guy I've ever met, that has a tire hanging from a rope in his office! (Johnny Carson)

This is a man who never forgets a friend. (Pause) But then he only has two!

This is a man who has absolutely no prejudice. (Long pause) He hates everyone equally!

This is a guy who goes to his family reunion, (Long pause) to meet women!

This is a guy who will wind up with a job with his name on his shirt!

This is a man you treat like your own father. (Long pause) You ignore him!

Charlie has given us a lot of pleasure at our house. (Long pause) He doesn't come over anymore! (Lucille Ball)

This is a man who was inducted into the House of Wax! (Long pause) As is! (Red Buttons)

Charlie is to comedy what surfing is to the economy of Nebraska!

Talk about a loser, this is a man who opened a bar in Watts. (Long pause) And named it Whiteys! (Leo Deurocher)

Charlie worked in a pet store. (Long pause) People kept asking, (Pause) "How big will he get?"

You know Charlie it's tough to make a comeback (Long pause) when you haven't been anywhere!

Charlie started out with nothing. (Long pause) And he still has most of it!

How do you get a Stanford graduate (or any school) off your porch? (Long pause) Pay him for the Pizza!

He has a personalized license plate. (Long pause) His dad made it!

His lifetime goal is to own a fireworks stand!

They no longer serve ice at Stanford games. (Or any school) (Pause) The senior who knew the recipe graduated!

Talk about paranoid. (Pause) He has a rear view mirror (Pause) on his stationary bike! (Richard Lewis)

He has a really deep voice. He's a basso profundo. (Long pause) This basso (Long pause) is the poster boy for the Massage Parlor Foundation!

Will Rogers once said, "I never met a man I didn't like!" (Long pause) Well he obviously never met Charlie!

I gave him a copy of the Joy Of Sex. (Pause) He took out his crayons and colored it! (Milton Berle)

I love this woman's laugh. When she laughs (Long pause) geese all over the world change direction!

His junior prom had a day care!

Put a straight jacket on him and you can take him anywhere!

He has all the warmth of a drumbeater on a slave ship!

I keep telling Charlie, I respect your position on the subject. (Long pause) It's you I don't like!

This is a man who never graduated from grammar school, high school or college. (Long pause) He has managed to stay stupid his entire life!

This is a man who is committed. (Long pause) At least he should be! (Dean Martin)

This was a man who (Pause) throughout the entire recession was able to keep his head above water. (Long, long pause) Well, (Long pause) wood floats!

She doesn't go out much. Actually, (Long pause) she has been stood up more often than a bowling pin!

This is a woman who had her goldfish fixed!

This is a man who plays strip solitaire!

The other day Charlie said to me, "You know, I'm nobody's fool." I said, "That's too bad, (Long pause) maybe we can get someone to adopt you!"

If this man cornered the mistletoe market, (Long pause) they would postpone Christmas!

I've seen his girlfriend and she isn't very attractive. Her ears are too big. (Long, long pause) She looks like a taxi with both doors open!

The other day he went to a mind reader. (Long pause) She charged him half price!

She could cook naked in a lumber camp, (Long pause) and no one would touch her!

She's kind of slow moving tonight. She was hurt taking a milk bath. (Long pause) The cow slipped (Pause) and fell on her head!

What a swinger this girl is. (Long pause) She bought her wedding dress in the sporting goods department!

This is a man who had to take remedial sand pile!

Talk about a lousy housekeeper. I bought her a vacuum cleaner. (Long pause) It threw up!

She looks like a million dollars tonight doesn't she? (Long, long pause) After taxes!

She gets brochures from nursing homes (Long pause) marked, "Urgent!"

Well, I have no doubt that Charlie is trying. (Long pause) He's very trying!

He played Hamlet. (Long pause) Hamlet lost!

She looks like a professional blind date!

In school, the kids called him chocolate bar. (Long pause) Because he was half nuts!

The good news is he's taking lessons in deportment. (Long pause) In about two weeks, (Long pause) he'll be deported!

This man can creep into your heart and soul. He can creep into your mind. (Pause) As a matter of fact, (Long pause) you'll never find a bigger creep in your whole life!

He was 25 years old before he could wave goodbye!

In college he was on the tug-of-war team. (Long, long pause) He was the forth jerk from the end!

She started out with a photographic mind. (Long pause) But it never developed!

It's been said that she has an early American face. (Long pause) She looks like George Washington!

This guy has all the personality (Pause) of a pound of wet liver!

This woman has hazel eyes, chestnut hair and walnut skin. (Long pause) She's a nut!

What a rocket scientist we have here tonight. He changed his name to Hilton (Pause) so it would be the same as his towels!

I knew she was here tonight. (Long pause) I saw the broom in the parking lot!

If you wanted to build an idiot, (Long pause) he would be the blueprint!

This is a responsible man. (Long pause) Every time something goes wrong (Long pause) he's responsible!

In "Who's Who" he's listed under "What's What!"

Charlie has proved that you are never too old (Long pause) to be stupid!

He likes to tinker around the house. As a matter of fact, (Long pause) people say he's the biggest tinker in town!

This is a man who doesn't know the meaning of the word quit. (Long pause) And there are a lot of other words he doesn't know the meaning of!

Look at him. (Long pause) I think the only reason he's walking around is to avoid funeral expenses!

His checking account is a disaster. (Long pause) He even had to give the bank back the toaster!

When this man is alone with his thoughts, (Long, long pause) he is really alone!

This man used to work in a coffee mill. (Long, long pause) But he couldn't stand the grind!

There's not enough meat on you to make a dog a bowl of soup! (L. Page)

What a pain in the butt this guy is! He's the kind of guy who goes to an orgy (Long pause) and complains about the grapes!

RECEIVING AN AWARD

Thank you for your support. (Long pause) I'll wear it until the day I die! (Dean Martin)

"I really don't deserve this. (Long pause) But I have arthritis and I don't deserve that either!" (Jack Benny)

This is an honor that comes to a man (Pause) maybe once in a lifetime. (Long pause) But why me?

I don't believe anyone has ever been so honored as I have been tonight. (Long, long pause) With the possible exception of when the Roman Senate threw a surprise party for Julius Caesar! (Hubert Humphrey)

I am humbled by the honor you paid me tonight. (Long, long pause) However, (Pause) I fully understand that if the plan tonight, (Pause) would have been to hang me, (Long pause) the crowd would have been twice as big!

RELIGION

He's at the age where any money he gives the church is no longer considered a donation. (Long pause). It's an investment!

The lion and the calf shall lie down together, (Pause) but the calf won't get much sleep!

Charlie was delivering his sermon and the guy in the back row yells, "I can't hear." (Long pause) A guy in the front row yells, "I can, I'll switch with you!"

He's a man who's done a lot for the Protestants! (Long pause) Because he's a Catholic!

Charlie doesn't always believe everything verbatim in the Bible. I mean he believed that Jesus really did walk on water! (Long pause) But it was January!

In the middle of his service, Charlie called out, "I ask you, (Pause) what must we do before we can ask the Lord to forgive our sins?" A voice booms out (Long pause), "Sin!"

He's an Episcopalian. That's an almost Catholic! (Pause) It means you can eat meat on Friday, (Long pause) but not a really good cut!

Our preacher welcomes all denominations, (Long pause) but he prefers twenties!

Charlie decides to go to Rome to see the Pope. He wants the Pope to make him a Cardinal. (Pause) That way, we'll only have to kiss his ring!

Here's a man who truly speaks to God. (Pause) Not in prayer, (Pause) but on a one to one! (Milton Berle)

This is a man who calls dial-a-prayer to see if he has any messages! (Milton Berle)

Billy Graham once said of this man, (Long pause) "There but for the grace of me, goes God!"

Everyone knows Charlie is Catholic. He's really into it. He's got so many candles in his house (Long pause) he can't even get fire insurance!

A little lad who was asked what we learn from the story of Jonah and the whale. He responded knowingly, (Pause) "People make whales sick!"

Times are really changing. I was so surprised at the selection of a Polish Pope, I called up our new priest and said, "Did you hear the news?" (Long pause) And she said!!!!

Water pollution is so bad today it takes real courage to be a skin diver, (Long pause) or a Baptist!

As the head of any church Board of Trustees will tell you, after all is said and done, (Pause) there's a lot more said than done!

America has become so tense and nervous it has been years since I've seen anyone asleep in church. And that is a sad situation! (Norman Vincent Peale)

A minister glared at one of his parishioners, "I understand you went to a ball game Sunday instead of to church." "That's a lie, preacher, (Pause) and I've got the fish to prove it!"

Somebody figured it out. We have 35 million laws (Pause) trying to enforce Ten Commandments!

I asked six year old Patrick, "Do you say a prayer before you eat?" The kid said, "I don't have to. (Pause) My mother's a good cook!"

Charlie started off life a little slowly. He was 16 before he knew that Holy Water was free!

Here's a guy who only found out last week that St. Christopher didn't have magnetic feet!

This is a man who told Billy Graham (Pause) he liked his crackers! (Foster Brooks)

I asked the good father, I said, "How do you get holy water?" He said, (Pause) "You boil the hell out of it!"

The bible tells us that Jesus was a Jew! (Pause) So how did he get a Mexican name?

He has been compared by some to St. Paul. (Long pause) One of the dullest cities in the country! (Dean Martin)

Until I was 8 years old, I thought my name was Jesus Christ! Everything my dad said started with, (Pause) "Jesus Christ you didn't do that again!"

Have you heard about that new Religion? It's called Jehovah's Standbys. (Pause) That's a Witness who doesn't want to get involved!

The Pope is the most loved man in the history of the world. (Pause) Nobody agrees with him, (Pause) but they all love him!

The difference between Jews and Catholics is that Jews are born with guilt. (Long pause) Catholics have to learn it in school! (Elayne Boosler)

I'll never understand how you can start with Adam and Eve, the most handsome and beautiful people in the history of the world. (Long pause) So where did all these ugly people come from?

I really feel sorry for poor Moses. Coming all the way down from Mount Sinai with these two big stone tablets. (Long pause) And a hernia!

On Easter, I figured out what our church choir gave up for lent. (Long pause) Rehearsals!

My preacher asked me why I only went to the 11:00 am service on Sunday. I told him I tried the 8:00 and 9:30 AM service but I figured if he was going to preach the same sermon 3 times, (Long pause) by 11:00 AM he'd have it down!

I'll tell you how bad the water pollution problem is becoming. Over half of all scuba equipment sold in this country, (Long pause) goes to Baptists!

True volunteer work is when your wife has to explain to your kids that Daddy hasn't died! (Long pause) He just became Chairman of the Board of Trustees!

My church asks you so often for money, (Long pause) you're never sure if you're one of the flock or one of the fleeced!

My grandson said, "Grandpa, when is the Preacher going to finish?" I said, "Son, (Long pause) he is finished. (Pause) He just hasn't stopped!"

On his headstone it will say: Here lies Charlie Jones——an Atheist (Long pause) all dressed up and no place to go!

A little girl became restless as Charlie's sermon dragged on and on. Finally, she leaned over to her mother and said, (Long pause) "Mommy, if we give him the money, will he let us go!"

I can always tell the difference between a Methodist and a Baptist. (Long, long pause) Baptists won't wave to each other in a liquor store!

Our church has become quite progressive. Along with the wafer in communion, (Long pause) they also offer a salad bar!

Mormons are very organized. I had this neighbor who stocked canned goods in her basement, so she could be prepared for when Christ returns to Earth. (Long pause) Apparently, (Pause) what Christ is looking for is creamed corn! (Natasha Ahanin)

The little kids were coming out of Sunday school and one said, "Do you believe all that stuff about the devil?" The other one said, "It's just like Santa Clause. (Long pause) It's your old man!"

There are some who attend church only three times in their lives. (Long pause) When they are hatched, (Pause) matched, (Pause) and dispatched!

RESTAURANTS

Why does Sea World have a seafood restaurant? I'm halfway through my fish burger and I realize, oh my God (Long pause) I could be eating a slow learner! (Lynda Montgomery)

Being in the restaurant business, I learned the difference between a Norwegian (or any country) and a canoe? (Pause) A canoe will sometimes tip!

Charlie's restaurant is going "no frills" service. Yesterday I ordered a hot chocolate. (Pause) The waitress brought me a chocolate bar and a match!

I called the waiter over and I said, "Waiter, didn't I tell you well done?" He said, (Pause) "Why thank you for the nice complement!"

I'll tell you how bad business has been in this restaurant. (Pause) Last night I saw the owner stealing from the bartender!

It was Charlie who first acquainted me with the finer points of gourmet dining. (Pause) Ripple with fish (Pause) and Muscatel with meat!

If the government is serious about making food a weapon, (Pause) Charlie's restaurant could be another Manhattan Project!

Charlie told the waiter, "I certainly don't like all these flies." The waiter said, "Well, just pick out the one you like and I'll kill the rest!"

At Charlie's restaurant they've got things a little mixed up. (Pause) The food is frozen, (Long pause) and the help is fresh!

Charlie really understands marketing. At his restaurant he has soft lights, good wine, good food, (Long pause) and a strolling tuba player!

It's hard to describe the waiters in Charlie's restaurant. (Long pause) Picture a bunch of New York cab drivers (Pause) in aprons!

Customers expect restaurants to be all things to all people. The other day this woman calls Charlie's restaurant and says, "Do you deliver?" Charlie says, "Yes." She says, "Good, (Long pause) the pains are coming three minutes apart!"

I won't go so far as to say that Charlie's restaurant is overly expensive. I mean it is a great place to eat. (Long pause) And any restaurant (Pause) that can make the Fortune 500 (Pause) deserves respect!

Charlie's restaurant just oozes with class. (Long pause) They even have midgets serving the shrimp cocktails!

In his restaurant they have this great soup that they claim is just like mother used to make. (Long pause) Just before they took Dad to the hospital!

Some of the waiters in Charlie's restaurant are really rude and territorial. I asked one guy what time it was. He said, (Long pause) "This isn't my table!"

I was in Charlie's restaurant and I said, "Waiter, do you have frog legs?" He said, "No sir, (Long pause) I sprained my knee so I've been walking like this!"

Charlie's restaurant isn't cheap. Yesterday I went in and paid $6.00 for a wing and a drumstick. It's the first time (Long pause) I ever paid an arm and a leg (Long pause) for an arm and a leg!

RETIREMENT

I am delighted to be here tonight. I know Charlie's delighted to be here. (Pause) At his age and in his condition, (Pause) he's delighted to be anywhere!

Tonight we honor a man who throughout his many years with the company was never too busy to see anyone. (Long pause) Mostly because he was never too busy!

Tonight we honor a man who, busy as he is, has always been able to find the time to listen to our problems, (Long pause) and then add to them!

Talk about his reputation as a ladies man. When he announced his retirement, (Pause) half the motels in America flew their sheets at half-mast! (Orson Wells)

Charlie told me he was fixed for life! (Long, long pause) I don't know if he means he has a pension plan (Pause) or just what!

Remember, Charlie, when you're retired (Pause) money is like sex. (Pause) You have to make a little bit go a long way!

Now that Charlie's retired, he's going out to learn a trade. (Long pause) So he'll know what kind of work he's out of!

I don't want to shake up our guest of honor, but you'll notice the saddest face at this retirement dinner, (Pause) is his wife's!

Retirement is when you're still filled with the vital juices of life, (Pause) only now they're prune!

Charlie retired but he still works most of the time. Betty told him, "I married you for better or for worse, (Pause) but not for lunch!"

His fellow employees tell me that this is a man who throughout his entire career did the work of two men. (Long pause). Laurel and Hardy!

Tonight we honor our leader for these many years. To share an evening, some drinks and even a meal together, (Pause) pretending that we like him!

Our man of the hour tonight is living proof that dedication, attention to detail, long hours and hard work, (Long pause) don't always work!

Charlie, this retirement isn't the end, it's the beginning. (Long pause) George Burns had pimples at your age!

Charlie, we've worked with you for many years and we don't know what we'll do without you. (Pause) But we've been dreaming about it for years!

Ralph told me that he plans to go places now that he's retired. That's good. (Pause) Because he certainly didn't go places while he worked for this company!

Retirement can be a happy time, a pleasant time, a wonderful time, (Long pause) unless you're married to Ralph!

He told me that after his retirement, he had seriously considered getting a vasectomy. But the doctor cautioned him, (Pause) "Let sleeping dogs lie!"

It was easy working for Charlie at the company. Each morning I'd come to work (Long pause) kiss his ring and go on from there!

ROTARY

Just remember, if you don't pitch in and do your part and we don't pitch in and do our part, (Pause) then more of us, (Long pause) won't have a part to pitch in! (Norm Crosby)

Charlie has been our president for one full year, a feat that would not have been possible without great sacrifice, (Long pause) by us!

I asked Charlie, if this club has any death benefits! He said, "Sure, (Pause) if you die you don't pay any more dues!"

Charlie, of course, is the President of our Rotary Club. (Pause) You can tell by eggshells all over his suit!

Charlie has come out strongly against the three-martini lunch. However, before he was president, (Pause) nobody drank that much!

Charlie, as our new club president, brings to us a new slogan that his company started using when he joined them. (Pause) "Seldom right but never in doubt!"

His fellow Rotarians will long remember Charlie for the job he's done this past year. (Long pause) Much as Nero was remembered by the early Christians!

Charlie told our Board last week that if he had money, he would travel. They took up a collection, (Pause) gave him 10 bucks, and told him to hit the road!

Charlie is a creative guy. He recently put a sign reading "Suggestion Box," (Pause) on the paper shredder!

Charlie, watching you run these meetings week in and week out, (Long pause) is like watching Stevie Wonder direct traffic!

Charlie has meant to Rotary, (Pause) what Henry Kissinger was to tap dancing!

He told me tonight that as our president, he was the architect of his own success. (Long pause) Lucky the building inspector didn't show up!

Our Rotary club just bought a new conference table for our board meetings. It's four feet wide, ten feet long, (Long pause) and sleeps twenty!

Charlie, watching you run these meetings week in and week out, is like watching a dog walking on his hind legs. (Long pause) He doesn't do it well, (Pause) but your amazed he can do it at all!

SALESMAN

This guy can tell you to go to hell so effectively, that you look forward to the trip!

Talk about confidence. If this guy went after Moby Dick, (Pause) it would be with a harpoon and a jar of tarter sauce!

Talk about a salesman. He's got Betty convinced (Pause) that polyester is the generic name for mink!

The first day on the job, the first day, he got two orders. (Pause) Get out and stay out!

This is the most incredible salesman I ever met! When he was courting Helen, he invited her up to his apartment to see his etchings! (Long pause) He sold her two of them!

I think this guy is the greatest salesman in the world! He's got his wife feeling sorry for the girl (Pause) who lost her bra and panties in his glove compartment!

What a salesman this guy is. He went to confession. (Long pause) The priest is now a bartender at the Pussy Cat in San Francisco!

What a salesman this guy is! His girl friend tried to talk him into buying her a dress. (Long pause) He talked her out of the one she was wearing!

This guy doesn't have it! (Long pause) He couldn't sell Blue Cross to Humpty Dumpty!

This guy is such a lousy salesman. (Long pause) He couldn't lure you out of a burning building!

SEVEN-ELEVEN'S

The other day I was at a 7-11 store, (Long pause) buying a few things for my friends! (Gary Shandling)

If the Iranian government ever calls out the Iranian National Guard, (Pause) they'll close every 7-11 in America!

SEX

Charlie told me the other day the true medical definition of a nymphomaniac. (Long pause) It's any woman with a sex drive greater than yours!

Charlie's interest in sex is waning! He's decided to save himself for special occasions! (Long pause) Like the installation of a new pope!

Charlie's brother came home early from work one day and saw a guy jogging naked. He said, "Why are you doing that?" The guy said, (Long pause) "Because you came home early!"

It's been said that Charlie here is one of the greatest lovers of the day! (Pause) His wife tells me that when night comes, (Pause) something leaves him!

My brother dates a homeless woman. (Pause) He says it's easier to talk her into staying over!

He went to a meeting of a support group for premature ejaculations. (Long pause). He left early!

A fellow said to his son. You must be very careful! Masturbation will make you blind!" The kid said, (Pause) "Hey dad, (Long pause) I'm over here!"

When I was very young, my dad taught me all about the birds and the bees! (Pause) He sure didn't know anything about sex!

She set some records in high school. (Pause). They said a girl couldn't make the football team! (Long pause) She did!

When I woke up this morning I felt like a 21-year-old. (Pause). But there's never one around when you need her!

In his day (Pause) safe sex meant you pushed the bed away from the wall so you wouldn't hit your head!

He told me tonight that it's been so long since he's had sex (Pause), he can't even remember which one gets tied up!

Charlie's sex life is so bad, (Pause) his self-winding watch stopped!

His pacemaker has been acting up lately. Every time he gets excited and has sex, (Pause) his garage door goes up!

He once went to a nudist wedding, (Pause) and came within an inch of being the best man!

In those days he didn't know much about girls (Pause), except what he could pick up!

This is a man who wanted to stay on at the honeymoon suite (Pause) as an instructor!

Bridegroom to the hotel clerk, "How much do we owe for the room?" "Five bucks apiece!" (Pause) He handed him fifty dollars.

My boss has a peculiar sense of humor. For my birthday he gave me an antique bed warmer. (Long pause) An eighty-year-old call girl!

Don't make love on an empty stomach. (Pause) Take her to dinner first!

His wife told me it only takes him 10 minutes to have sex. (Long pause) And that includes dinner and a show!

Ensign Pulver was the first man ever to be successful with a 50-year old maiden, because he was the first one ever to ask her a direct question!

You know it's a lot easier to tell a woman how wonderful it's going to be, (Pause) than how wonderful it was!

A fellow is stranded on a dessert island with six women. One day, another woman washes up on the beach. The guy says, "There go my Sundays!"

Charlie thinks about sex all the time. I was out shopping with him the other day. The clerk asked him what size hat he wore, and he says, "C cup!"

For it was Secretariat that once said, "Six million dollars and all I have to do is that?"

As a kid, for Christmas, Charlie always wanted a watch. (Long pause). His parents let him!!

Years ago, Charlie was once engaged to a very sexy contortionist. (Long pause) But she broke it off!

A new study just released by John Hopkins University has determined why it is that women don't blink during foreplay! (Long pause) They don't have time!

What do you call a girl who can suck a tennis ball through 25 feet of garden hose? (Long pause) "Precious!"

She traveled with the band. (Long pause) She wasn't a singer (Long pause) she just liked to travel with the band!

He takes Nytol and Vitamin E at the same time. He likes to sleep through his orgies!

She's got a sign on her desk that reads, "The buck stops here!" (Pause) She takes that very literally!

I met this really good-looking businesswoman in a bar. She said to me, "Do you really think I can make it big?" I said (Long pause), "You already have!"

He gave all his girl friends the same thing. (Long pause) Herpes!

Sex with a condom is not sex! (Long pause) It's Tupperware! (Paul Rodriguez)

When Charlie grew up, his town was so small they didn't have professional prostitutes. (Long pause) They had to make due with volunteers! (James Stewart)

Did you see the dress she wore yesterday? If it had been any shorter (Long pause) it would have been a collar!

The latest survey indicates there are 190 (Whatever number fits) prostitutes in our city. (Long, long pause) Of course these are loose figures!

You've got to be careful with the sexual harassment stuff these days. Yesterday one of our accounting girls came into my office and said she wanted to get something off her chest. (Long pause) I said, "What?" She said, (Pause) "The auditor!"

Despair is having a girl say yes, (Pause) and the motel desk clerk say no!

A loser is a guy who checks out of a motel with a girl friend, (Pause) and discovers that the desk clerk is Allan Funt of Candid Camera!

SHOPPING

My wife has two basic complaints. (Pause) First she has nothing to wear and second (Pause), she needs more closet space!

My wife holds a black belt in shopping!

I recently changed my will. I'm going to be buried in Nordstrom's parking lot, (Pause) so my wife will visit me three times a week!

A thief stole Helen's credit card. Charlie didn't report it. (Long pause) The thief was spending less than she was!

Talk about a shopper! You put up a sign that says 20% off, (Pause) and my wife will crawl across Antarctica on her hands and knees!

For his wife's birthday, Charlie went down to buy her a pair of Capri pants. (Long pause) But he didn't know how big her Capri was!

I was in a gift shop in an Indian reservation. The clerk told me a real Indian made the clay pot I was looking at. I said, "On the bottom of this thing it says, Made in Cleveland!" He says, (Long pause) "You never heard of the Cleveland Indians?"

I don't understand. My wife has a whole closet full of clothes that are too good to throw away (Long pause) but not good enough to wear!

Talk about a shopper. This woman was sick for a week (Long pause) and Saks Fifth Avenue went into bankruptcy!

This woman brings more bills into the house than a Congressman!

My wife is very punctual. (Long pause) She buys everything on time!

SHORT

Just remember, Charlie, short people get a lot more out of dancing with Raquel Welch!

After he saw Roots, he went to Ireland to trace his family tree. (Pause) As it turned out, (Pause) it was a stump! (L. Page)

He's never been to Venice. (Long pause) He's afraid he'd be mugged by a pigeon!

He was offered a job (Pause) in a piggy bank!

SPEAKER

Now I want you to understand folks that I'm not here tonight as an expert on any intellectual subject. (Pause) We'll start off even!

(If a joke falls flat) Here's another one you might not like! (Milton Berle)

Have you ever heard him talk before? He can speak 200 words a minute, (Pause) with gusts up to 350!

I have talked about as long as it seems!

The mind can absorb only what the bottom will endure!

Since early childhood, Charlie wanted to become a speaker in the worst way. (Long pause). He made it!

I would like to say this about Charlie. Any pasture that he's in (Pause) has got to be a little bit greener!

He can speak for an hour without a note, (Pause) and without a point!

(When you or someone else can't remember something) They say that the memory is the second thing that goes!

Do you ever sit through a meeting and get the feeling that we are busy (Pause) arranging the deck chairs on the Titanic!

I'm generally not an after-dinner speaker. (Pause) I'm not invited to dinner often enough to practice!

I know a lot of wives think that conventions are nothing but wine, women, and song, but that's not true. (Long pause) Not once have I heard one of you people sing!

(If someone asks a long and confusing question) That's a very meaty question. (Long pause) Baloney would seem to fit!

(Take off your watch and put it on the lectern.) Don't let that reassure you. (Long pause) It's a sundial!

(To a confused looking woman following a joke) He'll explain it to you later, madam!

(If it appears the audience is becoming confused) I don't think I'm getting through here. (Pause) It might be easier to explain integration to a lynch mob!

He held the audience in the palms of his hands. (Long pause) You could!

(To a person dragging out a question) Sir, would you mind just phrasing your question? Our lease is up in January!

(To a member of the audience asking a long, long question) I want to thank you for adding something to this program. (Pause, looking at your watch) About five minutes!

Ladies and Gentlemen, there are two classes of people in the world. (Pause) There are those who constantly divide the people of the world in two classes, (Long pause) and those who do not!

I said, "Charlie how did you get that audience of women to be so quiet?" He said, "It's easy. (Pause) Just tell them you'll take their questions, (Long pause) beginning with the oldest person first!"

I understand that the amount of sleep required by the average person is about an hour more than they get. (Long pause) I would appreciate it if you didn't pick up that missing hour during my talk tonight!

SPORTS

What a competitor this guy is. In a masturbation contest, (Pause) he'd come in first, third and eighth!

If you're a baseball fan, October is when you discover (Pause) your wife left you in May!

Here's a man who thought the St. Louis Cardinals (Pause) were appointed by the pope?

I have decided to take up cross-country skiing. I've been spending a lot of time looking at maps. (Long pause) Well I want to start out with a really small country!

She's a baseball widow. (Long, long pause) She hit her husband with a bat!

I think my wife used to be a baseball umpire. (Long pause) She makes quick decisions. (Pause) Never reverses them, (Long pause) and she doesn't think I'm safe when I'm out!

This team has been in the cellar so long (Long pause) that they spend most of their time growing mushrooms!

"It's not how you play the game it's only if you win," (Long pause) is the motto of Red China, Russia (Long pause) and Little League parents!

Skiing has brought happiness and joy to thousands of people. (Long pause) Those people are called (Pause) doctors!

This is a man who during his baseball career was thrown out 54 times at home. (Long pause) Three times on the baseball diamond (Pause) and 51 times at home!

His father was a professional baseball player. (Long pause) And Charlie was his first error!

This is a man who won an Olympic Gold Medal (Long pause) and had it bronzed!

There are three things you must learn if you plan to ski. How to put skis on, how to jump (Long pause) and how to walk again!

STOCK BROKER

What a financial wizard this guy is. He bought Zerox at 24 (Long pause) and sold it when he was 25!

Charlie is a broker. Broker, (Pause) that's the guy on the right end of the telephone!

Charlie is my broker and for years he has been telling me that Wall Street and Las Vegas have nothing to do with each other. (Long pause) So how come this week (Pause) he put a lounge show in his office?

They used to tell you that you can't take it with you. (Long pause) So how come my broker just opened an office at Forest Lawn?

This is a man who made a killing in the stock market. (Long, long pause) He shot his broker!

This recent stock market thing is ridiculous. I'm no longer a bull or a bear. (Long pause) I'm a chicken!

I'm worried. The other day I called my broker and told him to buy me 1,000 shares of I.B.M. (Long pause) He asked me how to spell it!

My broker called and told me that little men are back in the market. I asked him what that meant and he said, (Long pause) "Midgets are buying!"

My broker had me put $50,000 into a holding company and I finally discovered what they're holding. (Long pause) My $50,000!"

TOUGH NEIGHBORHOOD

His school was so tough that when the kids had their class picture taken, (Pause) they took both front and side shots!

When Charlie was a kid, he lived in such a poor and tough neighborhood that he used to play cops and robbers. (Long pause) With real cops!

Talk about living in a tough neighborhood. (Pause) The Christian Science Reading Room had a bouncer!

I lived in a tough neighborhood. You could walk ten blocks, (Pause) and never leave the scene of a crime!

Charlie went to a really tough high school. (Pause) His school newspaper had an obituary column!

Talk about a tough neighborhood. Everyone in the building next door is paying for protection. (Long pause) And that's a police station!

TRAVEL

For it was Orville Wright who turned to his brother and said, "We were in the air for 6 minutes and my luggage went to Seattle?"

He just returned from a trip. He was in Mexico (Long pause) for the Kaopectate festival!

I was in London when it was spring! I missed it! (Pause) I overslept!

I won't say that the airplane I arrived on today was small, (Long pause) but we dusted crops on the way in!

This plane is fully automated and nothing can possibly go wrong – go wrong – go wrong.

If you're beginning to look like your passport picture, (Pause) you need to take a trip!

He met Helen (His wife) at a travel agency. She was looking for a vacation, (Long pause) and he was the last resort!

Travel can bring you something you may have never experienced before. (Long pause) Poverty!

I called the airlines yesterday and said, "What's the fare to New York?" The guy said, "$300.00!" I said, "That's too much!" He said, (Long pause) "Let's talk!"

I always wondered why everyone in England drinks tea, (Long pause) until I tasted their coffee!

He went to Europe but he got hurt. (Long pause) He went jogging in Venice!

Did you folks come in on Amtrak? It's a wonderful train and it ranks right up there with the greats. (Long, long pause) Right after Lionel!

UGLY

Charlie was not an attractive child. When he was 6 years old, he was poster boy, (Pause) for Planned Parenthood!

Charlie claims that he's a man who has never gone to bed with an ugly woman. (Pause) He freely admits that he's woken up with a lot of ugly women!

He was an ugly kid. When he played in the sand box (Long pause) the cat kept covering him up!

Your mama is so ugly, she went to the beauty shop (Pause) and it took three hours (Long pause) for an estimate!

He's so ugly (Long Pause) every time he passes a bathroom the toilet flushes!

I wouldn't say she was ugly. I would say she had early American features. (Long pause) She looked like a Buffalo!

This is the only woman in America who can watch a tennis match without moving her head!

You talk about ugly. She got on a bus the other day (Long pause) and the driver quit!

UNLUCKY

He couldn't get lucky in a women's prison with a fist full of pardons! (Joey Bishop)

This is a man whose Karate instructor got beat up by a hairdresser! (Nippsy Russell)

Someone stole his watchdog! (Nippsy Russell)

Talk about unlucky. I had lunch with him the other day at a Chinese restaurant. When he opened the fortune cookie, (Pause) he got a subpoena!

Talk about unlucky! He just bought a new watch. It's shatter proof, water proof and anti-magnetic. (Long pause) He lost it!

He was once shipwrecked on a desert island with a woman! (Pause) And it was his wife!

Talk about unlucky. He picked up a prostitute the other day, (Pause) and she had a headache!

He played Monopoly (Pause) and got mugged on Boardwalk!

He is the kind of guy who buys a suit with 2 pair of pants. (Pause) Then burns a hole in the coat!

He gave up wine, women and song (Pause) and got run over by a truck!

In Reno, I watched him lose $42.00 in a gumball machine!

If Noah had lived today, he wouldn't have built an ark. (Pause) He would have put Charlie in charge of rain!

If he had been a rabbit on Noah's ark, the other rabbit (Pause) would have been named Bruce!

He has a canary that hums!

His dermatologist has acne!

When the meek inherit the earth, Charlie will get Little Rock!

He's had the 7-year itch for 8 years!

Talk about unlucky, (Long pause) his artificial flower died!

Talk about unlucky, health food (Long pause) makes him sick!

Talk about unlucky, (Long pause) his swimming pool burned down!

When he carried his wife over the threshold, (Long pause) he got a hernia!

Talk about unlucky, yesterday (Long pause) the Good Humor Man yelled at him!

Charlie's been having a string of bad luck. He has eight accounts that have gone bad, (Long pause) and a secretary who won't!

Talk about unlucky. I was sitting at home the other night reading my book while my wife did her crossword puzzle. She said, "What's a female sheep?" I said, "Ewe!" (Long pause) All hell broke loose!

His bank safety deposit box (Long pause) is missing!

The spare in his trunk blew out!

VETERINARIAN

My vet has a sign he hangs on his door when he steps out. It says, "Back in 10 minutes, Sit—Stay!"

He also has a sign in his waiting room that says, "Unattended children will be given free kittens!"

ABOUT THE AUTHOR

Allan Fisher was born in San Jose, California in 1934, the third of four children born to Elliott and Margaret Fisher. His father was a Methodist minister, his mother, an immigrant from Scotland.

Allan received a Bachelor's Degree in Marketing from Fairleigh Dickenson University in Rutherford, New Jersey and spent two years in graduate study at San Jose State University in California. He entered the healthcare industry in 1964 and shortly thereafter, became President of a chain of hospitals. Since then, he has continuously served as either President or Chairman of some of the larger healthcare companies in the country.

In addition to healthcare, Allan is heavily involved with the Boy Scouts of America. He became a member of the National Executive Board in 1985 and is the recipient of the Scouts' highest volunteer award, the Silver Buffalo.

Over the years, Allan has had considerable experience in motivational speaking. He acquired his love of humor from his father, along with the sense for "timing" that is all-important to a humorist. He has also served as MC at an untold number of Rotary Demotion roasts and Scouting functions around the country.

Following the publishing of "The Roast Book," a 500-page collection of short and longer stories, many readers indicated they weren't very good at telling longer stories but they could handle the one and two liners. This collection of his best one and two liners was designed to provide quick, hard-hitting material to meet that demand.

Enjoy!